P9-DIA-374

CHARLES BAUDELAIRE

RITTER LIBRARY
BALDWIN-WALLACE COLLEGE

Modern Critical Views

These and other titles in preparation

PQ 2191 .Z5 C434 1987
Charles Baudelaire

Modern Critical Views

CHARLES BAUDELAIRE

Edited and with an introduction by

Harold Bloom
Sterling Professor of the Humanities
Yale University

CHELSEA HOUSE PUBLISHERS ◇ 1987
New York ◇ New Haven ◇ Philadelphia

© 1987 by Chelsea House Publishers, a division of Chelsea
House Educational Communications, Inc.,
  95 Madison Avenue, New York, NY 10016
  345 Whitney Avenue, New Haven, CT 06511
  5014 West Chester Pike, Edgemont, PA 19028

Introduction © 1987 by Harold Bloom

All rights reserved. No part of this publication may be
reproduced or transmitted in any form or by any means
without the written permission of the publisher.

Printed and bound in the United States of America

∞ The paper used in this publication meets the minimum
requirements of the American National Standard for
Permanence of Paper for Printed Library Materials,
Z39.48-1984.

Library of Congress Cataloging-in-Publication Data
Charles Baudelaire.
    (Modern critical views)
    Bibliography: p.
    Includes index.
    1. Baudelaire, Charles, 1821–1867—Criticism and
interpretation.   I. Bloom, Harold.   II. Series.
PQ2191.Z5C434   1987   841'.8   86-24464
ISBN 0-87754-719-X (alk. paper)

Contents

Editor's Note

This book brings together a representative selection of the best modern criticism devoted to Baudelaire, reprinted here in the chronological order of its original publication. I am grateful to Olga Popov for her erudition and judgment in helping me to edit this volume.

My introduction considers Baudelaire's ambivalent relationship to his Romantic precursor, Victor Hugo, and then speculates upon Baudelaire's poems of Lesbian love. The chronological sequence of criticism begins with an essay by Georges Bataille, who, seeking to explain Baudelaire's denial of the Good, sees it as a rejection of the future, a turning away from rebellion in order to extract strength from deliberate failure.

Interpreting "La Chevelure," Victor Brombert illuminates Baudelaire's dialectic of intoxication-as-experience and intoxication-as-method. Brombert's thematic approach contrasts with Barbara Johnson's deconstructions of the two "Invitations au voyage," prose and verse. A third critical mode, emphasizing consciousness as the interpretive center, is exemplified here by Georges Poulet, who finds Baudelaire's intellect defining itself "either as pure depth without objects, or as pure activity of mind without reason or end."

Rosemary Lloyd, describing Baudelaire's literary criticism, sees it as crossing the line between "creative criticism" and the prose poem. In a study of the relation between *La Fanfarlo* and the *Salon de 1846*, Bernard Howells sketches Baudelaire in 1846, a portrait of the artist as a young man. A third essay upon the dialectic of criticism and creation in Baudelaire is provided by Mary Ann Caws, who juxtaposes Baudelaire's translation of Poe's tale, "The Oval Portrait," with Baudelaire's own poem, "Un Fantôme."

Paul de Man, one of the supreme modern critics, reads Baudelaire's sonnet, "Correspondances," and his lyric, "Obsession," as instances of tropological processes at work mystifying us, thus demonstrating to us the gap in all poems between rhetoric-as-persuasion and rhetoric-as-trope.

This book ends with a previously unpublished essay on temporality in Baudelaire by Helen Regueiro Elam, who supplements de Man by finding in Baudelaire the radical gap between the demand for a transcendence of mere metaphor, and an actual intensification of metaphor in the major poems.

Introduction

I

Sartre ended his book on Baudelaire by insisting that this poet, like Emerson's ideal being, made his own circumstances:

> But we should look in vain for a single circumstance for which he was not fully and consciously responsible. Every event was a reflection of that indecomposable totality which he was from the first to the last day of his life. He refused experience. Nothing came from outside to change him and he learned nothing.

Could there have been such a person? Can any poet refuse the experience of reading his precursors? Was Victor Hugo a circumstance for which Baudelaire was fully and consciously responsible? Valéry, who was (unlike Sartre) a theorist of poetic influence, thought otherwise:

> Thus Baudelaire regarded Victor Hugo, and it is not impossible to conjecture what he thought of him. Hugo reigned; he had acquired over Lamartine the advantage of infinitely more powerful and more precise *working materials*. The vast range of his diction, the diversity of his rhythms, the superabundance of his images, crushed all rival poetry. But his work sometimes made concessions to the vulgar, lost itself in prophetic eloquence and infinite apostrophes. He flirted with the crowd, he indulged in dialogues with God. The simplicity of his philosophy, the disproportion and incoherence of the developments, the frequent contrasts between the marvels of detail and the fragility of the subject, the inconsistency of the whole—everything, in a word, which could shock and thus instruct and orientate a pitiless young observer toward his future personal art—all these things Baudelaire was to note in himself and separate from the admiration

forced upon him by the magic gifts of Hugo, the impurities, the imprudences, the vulnerable points in his work—that is to say, the possibilities of life and the opportunities for fame which so great an artist left to be gleaned.

With some malice and a little more ingenuity than is called for, it would be only too tempting to compare Victor Hugo's poetry with Baudelaire's, with the object of showing how exactly *complementary* the latter is to the former. I shall say no more. It is evident that Baudelaire sought to do what Victor Hugo had not done; that he refrained from all the effects in which Victor Hugo was invincible; that he returned to a prosody less free and scrupulously removed from prose; that he pursued and almost always captured the production of *unbroken charm*, the inappreciable and quasi-transcendent quality of certain poems—but a quality seldom encountered, and rarely in its pure state, in the immense work of Victor Hugo. . . .

Hugo never ceased to learn by practice; Baudelaire, the span of whose life scarcely exceeded the *half* of Hugo's, developed in quite another manner. One would say he had to compensate for the probable brevity and foreshadowed insufficiency of the short space of time he had to live, by the employment of that critical intelligence of which I spoke above. A score of years were vouchsafed him to attain the peak of his own perfection, to discover his personal field and to define a specific form and attitude which would carry and preserve his name. Time was lacking to realize his literary ambitions by numerous experiments and an extensive output of works. He had to choose the shortest road, to limit himself in his gropings, to be sparing of repetitions and divergences. He had therefore to seek by means of analysis what he was, what he could do, and what he wished to do; and to unite, in himself, with the spontaneous virtues of a poet, the sagacity, the skepticism, the attention and reasoning faculty of a critic.

One can transpose this simply enough into very nearly any of the major instances of poetic influence in English. Attempt Wallace Stevens, a true peer of Valéry, but with a more repressed or disguised relation to Whitman than Baudelaire manifested towards Hugo:

It is evident that Wallace Stevens sought to do what Walt Whitman had not done; that he refrained from all the effects in which Walt Whitman was invincible; that he returned to a prosody less free and scrupulously removed from prose; that he pursued and almost always captured the production of *unbroken charm*, the inappreciable and quasi-transcendent quality of certain poems— but a quality seldom encountered, and rarely in its pure state, in the immense work of Walt Whitman.

Valéry, unlike both Formalist and Post-Structuralist critics, understood that Hugo was to French poetry what Whitman was to American poetry, and Wordsworth was to all British poetry after him: the inescapable precursor. Baudelaire's Hugo problem was enhanced because the already legendary poetic father was scarcely twenty years older than the gatherer of *Les Fleurs du Mal*. All French literary movements are curiously belated in relation to Anglo-American literature. Current French sensibility of the school of Derrida is merely a revival of the Anglo-American literary Modernism of which Hugh Kenner remains the antiquarian celebrant. "Post-Structuralist Joyce" is simply Joyce as we read and discussed him when I was a graduate student, thirty-five years ago. In the same manner, the French Romanticism of Hugo in 1830 repeated (somewhat unknowingly) the movement of British sensibility that produced Wordsworth and Coleridge, Byron and Shelley and Keats, of whom the first two were poetically dead, and the younger three long deceased, well before Hugo made his revolution.

Baudelaire started with the declaration that the Romanticism of 1830 could not be the Romanticism (or anything else) of 1845. T. S. Eliot, as was inevitable, cleansed Baudelaire of Romanticism, baptized the poet into an Original Sinner and a Neo-Classicist, and even went so far as to declare the bard of Lesbos a second Goethe. A rugged and powerful literary thinker, Baudelaire doubtless would have accepted these amiable distortions as compliments, but they do not help much in reading him now.

His attitude towards Hugo, always tinged with ambivalence, became at times savage, but a student of poetic influence learns to regard such a pattern as one of the major modes of misprision, of that strong misreading of strong poets that permits other strong poets to be born. *The Salon of 1845* blames the painter Boulanger on poor Hugo:

> Here we have the last ruins of the old romanticism—this is what it means to come at a time when it is the accepted belief that inspiration is enough and takes the place of everything else; this is the abyss to which the unbridled course of Mazeppa has led. It is M. Victor Hugo that has destroyed M. Boulanger—after having destroyed so many others; it is the poet that has tumbled the painter into the ditch. And yet M. Boulanger can paint de-

cently enough—look at his portraits. But where on earth did he win his diploma as history-painter and inspired artist? Can it have been in the prefaces and odes of his illustrious friend?

That Baudelaire was determined not to be destroyed by Hugo was clear enough, a determination confirmed by the rather invidious comparison of Delacroix to Hugo in *The Salon of 1846:*

> Up to the present, Eugène Delacroix has met with injustice. Criticism, for him, has been bitter and ignorant; with one or two noble exceptions, even the praises of his admirers must often have seemed offensive to him. Generally speaking, and for most people, to mention Eugène Delacroix is to throw into their minds goodness knows what vague ideas of ill-directed fire, of turbulence, of hazardous inspiration, of confusion, even; and for those gentlemen who form the majority of the public, pure chance, that loyal and obliging servant of genius, plays an important part in his happiest compositions. In that unhappy period of revolution of which I was speaking a moment ago and whose numerous errors I have recorded, people used often to compare Eugène Delacroix to Victor Hugo. They had their romantic poet; they needed their painter. This necessity of going to any length to find counterparts and analogues in the different arts often results in strange blunders; and this one proves once again how little people knew what they were about. Without any doubt the comparison must have seemed a painful one to Eugène Delacroix, if not to both of them; for if my definition of romanticism (intimacy, spirituality and the rest) places Delacroix at its head, it naturally excludes M. Victor Hugo. The parallel has endured in the banal realm of accepted ideas, and these two preconceptions still encumber many feeble brains. Let us be done with these rhetorical ineptitudes once and for all. I beg all those who have felt the need to create some kind of aesthetic for their own use and to deduce causes from their results to make a careful comparison between the productions of these two artists.
>
> M. Victor Hugo, whose nobility and majesty I certainly have no wish to belittle, is a workman far more adroit than inventive, a labourer much more correct than *creative*. Delacroix is sometimes clumsy, but he is essentially creative. In all his pictures, both lyric and dramatic, M. Victor Hugo lets one see a system of uniform alignment and contrasts. With him even eccentricity takes symmetrical forms. He is in complete possession of, and

coldly employs, all the modulations of rhyme, all the resources of antithesis and all the tricks of apposition. He is a composer of the decadence or transition, who handles his tools with a truly admirable and curious dexterity. M. Hugo was by nature an academician even before he was born, and if we were still living in the time of fabulous marvels, I would be prepared to believe that often, as he passed before their wrathful sanctuary, the green lions of the *Institut* would murmur to him in prophetic tones, "Thou shalt enter these portals."

For Delacroix justice is more sluggish. His works, on the contrary, are poems—and great poems, *naïvely* conceived and executed with the usual insolence of genius. In the works of the former there is nothing left to guess at, for he takes so much pleasure in exhibiting his skill that he omits not one blade of grass nor even the reflection of a street-lamp. The latter in his works throws open immense vistas to the most adventurous imaginations. The first enjoys a certain calmness, let us rather say a certain detached egoism, which causes an unusual coldness and moderation to hover above his poetry—qualities which the dogged and melancholy passion of the second, at grips with the obstinacies of his craft, does not always permit him to retain. One starts with detail, the other with an intimate understanding of his subject; from which it follows that one only captures the skin, while the other tears out the entrails. Too earthbound, too attentive to the superficies of nature, M. Victor Hugo has become a painter in poetry; Delacroix, always respectful of his ideal, is often, without knowing it, a poet in painting.

This is grand polemical criticism, deliciously unfair to the greatest French poet ever. Hugo is now adroit, but not inventive; a correct laborer, but not creative. Few critical remarks are as effectively destructive as: "with him even eccentricity takes symmetrical forms." Hugo is somehow a mere, earthbound painter of nature, and an academic impostor, doomed from birth to be an institutional pillar. Baudelaire's stance towards Hugo over the next decade became yet more negative, so that it is at first something of a surprise to read his letters to the exiled Hugo in 1859. Yet the complex rhetoric of the letters is again wholly human, all too human, in the agon of poetic influence:

So now I owe you some explanations. I know your works by heart and your prefaces show me that I've overstepped the theory you generally put forward on the alliance of morality and poetry.

But at a time when society turns away from art with such disgust, when men allow themselves to be debased by purely utilitarian concerns, I think there's no great harm in exaggerating a little in the other direction. It's possible that I've protested too much. But that was in order to obtain what was needed. Finally, even if there were a little Asiatic fatalism mixed up in my reflections I think that would be pardonable. The terrible world in which we live gives one a taste for isolation and fatality.

What I wanted to do above all was to bring the reader's thoughts back to that wonderful little age whose true king you were, and which lives on in my mind like a delicious memory of childhood. . . .

The lines I enclose with this letter have been knocking around in my brain for a long time. The second piece was written with the *aim of imitating you* (laugh at my absurdity, it makes me laugh myself) after I'd reread some poems in your collections, in which such magnificent charity blends with such touching familiarity. In art galleries I've sometimes seen wretched art students copying the works of the masters. Well done or botched, these imitations sometimes contained, unbeknownst to the students, something of their own character, be it great or common. Perhaps (perhaps!) that will excuse my boldness. When *The Flowers of Evil* reappears, swollen with three times as much material as the Court suppressed, I'll have the pleasure of inscribing at the head of these poems the name of the poet whose works have taught me so much and brought such pleasure to my youth.

"That wonderful little age" doubtless referred to the Romanticism of the Revolution of 1830, that enchanted moment when Victor Hugo was king. But the true reference is to the nine-year-old Baudelaire, who found in his precursor "a delicious memory of childhood," and no mere likeness. When Baudelaire goes on to speak of imitation he cannot forbear the qualification: "something of their own character, great or common." A few months later, sending his poem, "The Swan," to Hugo, he asked that the poem be judged "with your paternal eyes." But, a year later, Baudelaire again condemned Hugo for: "his concern with contemporary events . . . the belief in progress, the salvation of mankind by the use of balloons, etc."

The whip of ambivalence lashed back and forth in Baudelaire. Though a believer in salvation through balloons, the bardic Hugo was also, in his bad son's estimate, a force of nature: "No other artist is so universal in scope, more adept at coming into contact with the forces of the universe, more disposed to immerse himself in nature." That might seem definitive, but later Baudelaire allowed himself this diatribe, which hardly dents the divine precursor:

> Hugo thinks a great deal about Prometheus. He has placed an imaginary vulture on a breast that is never lacerated by anything more than the flea-bites of his own vanity . . .
>
> Hugo-the-Almighty always has his head bowed in thought; no wonder he never sees anything except his own navel.

It is painful to read this; more painful still to read the references to Hugo in Baudelaire's letters of 1865–66. One moment, in its flash of a healthier humor, renders a grand, partly involuntary tribute to the normative visionary who both inspired and distressed Baudelaire:

> It appears that he and the Ocean have quarreled! Either he has not the strength to bear the Ocean longer, or the Ocean has grown weary of his presence.

To confront, thus again, the rock-like ego of that force of nature, your poetic father, is to admit implicitly that he returns in his own colors, and not in your own.

II

Proust, in a letter to Jacques Rivière, compared Baudelaire to Hugo and clearly gave the preference to Baudelaire. What Wallace Stevens, following Baudelaire, called the profound poetry of the poor and of the dead, seemed to Proust wholly Baudelaire's, and not Hugo's. But as love poets, Hugo and Baudelaire seemed more equal, even perhaps with Hugo the superior. Proust said he preferred Hugo to Baudelaire in a great common trope:

> Elle me regarda de ce regard suprême
> Qui reste à la beauté quand nous en triômphons.

> She gazed at me with that supreme look
> Which endures in beauty even while it is vanquished.
>
> > (Hugo)

> Et cette gratitude infinie et sublime
> Qui sort de la paupière ainsi qu'un long soupir

> And that sublime and infinite gratitude
> which glistens under the eyelids like a sigh.
>
> > (Baudelaire)

Both tropes are superb; I too prefer Hugo's, but why did Proust have that preference, or pretend to have it? Both beauties have been vanquished, but Hugo's by the potent Victor himself, while Baudelaire's Hippolyta reflects the triumph of Delphine, who stares at her victim with the shining eyes of a lioness. Proust, perhaps rather slyly, says he prefers the heterosexual trope to the Lesbian one, but does not say why. Yet, superb critic that he was, he helps us to expand Valéry's insight. Resolving to do precisely what Hugo had not done, Baudelaire became the modern poet of Lesbos, achieving so complex a vision of that alternative convention of Eros as to usurp forever anyone else's representation of it:

> Comme un bétail pensif sur le sable couchées,
> Elles tournent leurs yeux vers l'horizon des mers,
> Et leurs pieds se cherchant et leurs mains rapprochées
> Ont de douces langueurs et des frissons amers.
>
> Les unes, coeurs épris de longues confidences,
> Dans le fond des bosquets où jasent les ruisseaux,
> Vont épelant l'amour des craintives enfances
> Et creusent le bois vert des jeunes arbrisseaux;
>
> D'autres, comme des soeurs, marchent lentes et graves
> A travers les rochers pleins d'apparitions,
> Où saint Antoine a vu surgir comme des laves
> Les seins nus et pourprés de ses tentations;
>
> Il en est, aux lueurs des résines croulantes,
> Qui dans le creux muet des vieux antres païens
> T'appellent au secours de leurs fièvres hurlantes,
> O Bacchus, endormeur des remords anciens!
>
> Et d'autres, dont la gorge aime les scapulaires,
> Qui, recélant un fouet sous leurs longs vêtements,
> Mêlent, dans le bois sombre et les nuits solitaires,
> L'écume du plaisir aux larmes des tourments.
>
> O vierges, ô démons, ô monstres, ô martyres,
> De la réalité grands esprits contempteurs,
> Chercheuses d'infini, dévotes et satyres,
> Tantôt pleines de cris, tantôt pleines de pleurs,
>
> Vous que dans votre enfer mon âme a poursuivies,
> Pauvres soeurs, je vous aime autant que je vous plains,
> Pour vos mornes douleurs, vos soifs inassouvies,
> Et les urnes d'amour dont vos grands coeurs sont pleins!

Pensive as cattle resting on the beach,
they are staring out to sea; their hands and feet
creep toward each other imperceptibly
and touch at last, hesitant then fierce.

How eagerly some, beguiled by secrets shared,
follow a talkative stream among the trees,
spelling out their timid childhood's love
and carving initials in the tender wood;

others pace as slow and grave as nuns
among the rocks where Anthony beheld
the purple breasts of his temptations rise
like lava from the visionary earth;

some by torchlight in the silent caves
consecrated once to pagan rites
invoke—to quench their fever's holocaust—
Bacchus, healer of the old regrets;

others still, beneath their scapulars,
conceal a whip that in the solitude
and darkness of the forest reconciles
tears of pleasure with the tears of pain.

Virgins, demons, monsters, martyrs, all
great spirits scornful of reality,
saints and satyrs in search of the infinite,
racked with sobs or loud in ecstasy,

you whom my soul has followed to your hell,
Sisters! I love you as I pity you
for your bleak sorrows, for your unslaked thirsts,
and for the love that gorges your great hearts!

Richard Howard's superb translation greatly assists my inner ear, inadequate for the nuances of Baudelaire's French, in the labor of apprehending what Erich Auerbach memorably spoke of as Baudelaire's aesthetic dignity, that all-but-unique fusion of Romantic pathos and classical irony, so clearly dominant in these immense quatrains. Yet I would place the emphasis elsewhere, upon that psychological acuity in which Baudelaire surpasses nearly all poets, Shakespeare excepted. Freud, speculating upon female homosexuality, uttered the grand and plaintive cry: "we find masculinity vanishing into activity and femininity into passivity, and that does not tell us enough."

Baudelaire does tell us enough, almost more than enough, even as Melanie Klein came, after Freud and Karl Abraham, to tell us much more than enough. The "damned women," really little children, play at being masculine and feminine, for Baudelaire's great insight is that Lesbianism transforms the erotic into the aesthetic, transforms compulsion into a vain play that remains compulsive. "Scornful of reality," and so of the reality principle that is our consciousness of mortality, Baudelaire's great spirits search out the infinite, and discover that the only infinity is the hell of repetition. One thinks back to Delphine and Hippolyta; Baudelaire sees and shows that Delphine is the daughter revenging herself upon the mother, even as Hippolyta revenges herself upon the mother in quite another way. When Hippolyta cries out: "Let me annihilate myself upon / your breast and find the solace of a grave!" then we feel that Baudelaire has made Melanie Klein redundant, perhaps superfluous. The revenge upon the mother is doubtless Baudelaire's revenge upon his own mother, but more profoundly it is the aesthetic revenge upon nature. In Baudelaire's own case, was it not also the revenge upon that force of nature, too conversant with ocean, that victorious poetic father, the so-often reviled but never forgotten Victor Hugo?

GEORGES BATAILLE

A Perfect Silence of the Will

MAN CANNOT LOVE HIMSELF TO THE END UNLESS HE CONDEMNS HIMSELF

Sartre has defined Baudelaire's moral position with the utmost precision [in his book *Baudelaire*].

> To do Evil for the sake of Evil is to do the exact opposite of what we continue to affirm is Good. It is to want what we do not want—since we continue to abhor the powers of Evil—and not to want what we want, for Good is always defined as the object and end of the deepest will. This was Baudelaire's attitude. Between his acts and those of the normal sinner there lay the same difference as between black magic and atheism. The atheist does not care about God because he has decided once and for all that He does not exist. But the priest of the black mass hates God because He is lovable; he scoffs Him because He is respectable; he sets himself to denying the established order, but, at the same time, preserves this order and asserts it more than ever. Were he for a moment to stop asserting it his conscience would return to peace with itself. Evil would suddenly turn into Good and, transcending all orders which do not emanate from himself, he would emerge in nothingness, without God, without excuses, having assumed his full responsibility.

From *Literature and Evil*, translated by Alastair Hamilton. © 1973 by Calder & Boyars Ltd.

This is undoubtedly true. Further on, Sartre's view is of still greater interest.

> In order for liberty to be complete it has to be offered the choice . . . of being infinitely wrong. It is therefore *unique* in this whole universe committed to Good, but it must adhere totally to Good, maintain it and strengthen it in order to be able to plunge into Evil. And he who damns himself acquires a solitude which is a feeble image of the great solitude of the truly free man. In a certain sense he creates. In a universe where each element sacrifices itself in order to converge in the greatness of the whole, he brings out the singularity, that is to say the rebelliousness of a fragment or a detail. Thus something appears which did not exist before, which nothing can efface and which was in no way prepared by worldly materialism. It becomes a work of luxury, gratuitous and unpredictable. Let us observe the relationship between Evil and poetry: when poetry goes as far as to take Evil as its object the two forms of creation, whose responsibility is essentially limited, meet and merge—we possess a flower of Evil. But the deliberate creation of Evil—that is to say, wrong—is acceptance and recognition of Good. It pays homage to it and, by calling itself wicked, it admits that it is relative and derivative—that it could not exist without Good.

Sartre also refers, in passing, to the relationship between Evil and poetry, but he draws no conclusions from it. The evil element is very apparent in Baudelaire's work, but is it connected with the essential nature of poetry? Sartre says nothing about this. He merely describes as liberty that possible state in which man is no longer supported by traditional Good—or by the established order. In comparison to this major position, he regards the poet's position as minor. Baudelaire "never went beyond the phase of childhood." "He defined genius as 'childhood regained at will.' " Childhood lives in faith.

> But if the child grows older, grows superior to his parents in intelligence and looks over their shoulder, (he may see that) behind them there is nothing. The duties, the rites, the precise and limited obligations suddenly disappear. Unjustified and unjustifiable, he suddenly experiences his terrible liberty. Everything has to be begun again: he suddenly emerges in solitude and nothingness. That was what Baudelaire wanted to avoid at all costs.

At one point in his study Sartre reproaches Baudelaire for having regarded "moral life as a constraint . . . and never as a tortured quest." But surely we can say of poetry—and not only of Baudelaire's poetry—that it is a "tortured quest" for a moral truth which it may have discovered by mistake? Sartre has unintentionally connected the ethical problem with the poetic problem. He quotes a passage from Baudelaire's letter to Ancelle, dated February 18, 1866. "Should I tell you, who have guessed it no more than the others, that I have put my whole heart, my whole affection, my whole religion (in disguise), my whole hatred, my whole misfortune into this atrocious book? It is true that I will write the contrary, that I will swear by the gods that it is a book of pure art, of imitation, of imposture, and I will be an arrant liar." Sartre includes this quotation in his proof that Baudelaire acknowledged the ethics of his judges and made *Les Fleurs du Mal* pass for a diversion (a work of Art for Art's sake) or for "an edifying work intended to instil in the reader a horror for vice." The letter to Ancelle undoubtedly makes better sense than the disguises. But Sartre has simplified a problem which calls into question the very basis of poetry and ethics.

If liberty—I must be allowed to state my proposition before I justify it—is the essential quality of poetry, and if free and sovereign behaviour deserves no more than a "tortured quest," the misery of poetry and the bonds imposed by liberty become evident. Though poetry may trample verbally on the established order, it is no substitute for it. When disgust with a powerless liberty thoroughly commits the poet to political action he abandons poetry. But he immediately assumes responsibility for the order to come: he asserts the direction of activity, the major attitude. When we see him we cannot help being aware that poetic existence, in which we once saw the possibility of a sovereign attitude, is really a minor attitude. It becomes no more than a child's attitude, a gratuitous game. Strictly speaking liberty would be the power of a child. For the adult, bound by the obligatory regulations of action, it would be a mere dream, a desire, a spectre. Is liberty not the power which God lacks, or which He only possesses verbally since He cannot disobey the order which *He is*, which He guarantees?

God's profound liberty disappears for the man in whose eyes Satan alone is free. "But who, basically, is Satan?" asks Sartre, "if not the symbol of disobedient and sulky children who want to remain as their parents see them and who do Evil within the bounds of Good in order to assert and consecrate it?" The liberty of the child (or the devil) is evidently limited by the adult (or by God), who turns it to mockery (who diminishes it). The child, therefore, nurtures feelings of hatred and rebelliousness restrained by admiration and envy. In so far as he approaches rebellion he assumes an adult's responsibility. He can, if he likes, blind himself in various ways. He can pretend to assume the major prerogatives of the adult, but without acknowledging the obligations connected with them—this would be the ingenuous attitude, the bluff which requires complete puerility. He can continue to lead a free life at the expense of those who are entertained by him— this limp form of liberty is traditionally the poet's prerogative. He can put other people off with fine words, or he can alleviate the weight of a prosaic reality by emphasising it. But there is both an air of imposture and an evil odour connected with these poor possibilities. If it is true that the impossible, which has, in a way, been chosen and therefore acknowledged, smells no less foul, and if the ultimate unsatisfaction (that with which the mind is satisfied) is itself a form of imposture, we can at least say that there is a privileged form of misery which admits itself to be such.

It is ashamed to admit itself to be such. The problem which Sartre unwittingly raises cannot easily be solved. If it is true that Baudelaire's attitude was in many ways unfortunate, it seems inhuman to hold it against him. Yet we would have no alternative if we were not to take into account the fact that Baudelaire deliberately refused to behave like a real man, that is to say, like a prosaic man. Sartre is right: Baudelaire chose to be wrong, like a child. But before we condemn him we must ask ourselves what sort of choice we are dealing with. Was it made for lack of anything else? Was it just a deplorable mistake? Or was it the result of excess? Was it made in a miserable but no less decisive manner? I even wonder whether such a choice is not essentially that of poetry? Is it not *the choice of man?*

This is the point of my book [*Literature and Evil*]. I believe that man is necessarily put up against himself and that he cannot recognise himself and love himself to the end unless he is condemned.

THE PROSAIC WORLD OF ACTIVITY AND THE WORLD OF POETRY

My previous propositions bring us to a world which I cannot blame Sartre for avoiding. My book is an attempt to discover this new world. But this will only appear gradually . . .

"If man did not shut his eyes in a sovereign manner," wrote René Char, "he would end up by no longer seeing things worth looking at." But, Sartre says

> For the rest of us, it is enough to see the tree or the house.
> Absorbed as we are in contemplating them, we forget ourselves.
> Baudelaire was the man who never forgot himself. He watched

himself seeing, he watched in order to see himself watching. It was his awareness of the tree or the house which he watched, and things only appeared to him through this awareness, paler, smaller, less touching, as though he saw them through a pair of opera glasses. They did not point to each other like a signpost or a book marker. . . . Their immediate mission was to bring the individual back to self-awareness. [And further on] There was an original distance between Baudelaire and the world, which is not ours. Between the objects and himself there was always a somewhat cloying lucidity, like a breath of warm summer air.

There is no better or more precise way of representing the distance between poetic vision and everyday life. We forget ourselves when the signpost points to the road or the marker shows us the page in a book. But this vision is not *sovereign:* it is subordinate to our search for the road (which we are about to take) or for the page (which we are about to read). In other words the present (the signpost or the book marker) is here determined by the future (the road or the page). According to Sartre, "it is the determination of the present by the future, of what exists by what does not yet exist . . . which philosophers today call transcendence." In as much as the signpost or the book marker have this transcendent significance they do admittedly suppress us and we forget ourselves if we look upon them in this subordinate manner. The "paler, smaller, less touching" things, on the other hand, to which Baudelaire opened his eyes *sovereignly*, did not suppress him for they served "no other purpose than to give him the opportunity of observing himself as he saw them. . . ."

If it is true that the poetic process wants the object to become the subject, the subject the object, would it be more than a game, a brilliant sleight of hand? Basically there can be no doubt about the possibility of poetry. But is the history of poetry a mere succession of futile efforts? We can hardly deny that, as a general rule, poets cheat! "Poets lie too much," says Zarathustra, who adds "Zarathustra himself is a poet." But the fusion of subject and object, of man and the world, cannot be feigned. We could avoid attempting it in the first place, but that would be absurd.

Such a fusion would appear to be impossible. Sartre rightly says, with regard to this impossibility, that the tragedy of the poet is due to the mad desire to unite the being and existence objectively. I have already said that, according to Sartre, this desire is, at times, that of Baudelaire in particular, and at others, that of "every poet." But whichever way we look at it the synthesis of the unchangeable and the perishable, of the being and existence, of the object and the subject, which poetry seeks, is an ultimate definition of poetry. It limits it and transposes it into the realm of the impossible and the unsatisfiable. Unfortunately it is difficult to talk of the impossible being condemned to existence. The recurrent theme of Sartre's study is that Baudelaire's misfortune was to want to be what he was for others: he thereby abandoned the prerogative of existence, which is to remain in abeyance. But does man tend to prevent his consciousness from becoming a thing like any other by letting it become a reflection of things? I do not think so. Poetry is the means by which, in his ignorance of the means Sartre has proposed to him, he can escape from being reduced to the reflection of things. It is true that poetry, in its quest for the identity of reflected things and the consciousness which reflects them, wants the impossible. But surely the very means of avoiding reduction to the reflection of things constitute a desire for the impossible.

IN A SENSE POETRY IS ALWAYS THE OPPOSITE OF POETRY

I believe that the misery of poetry is faithfully represented in Sartre's image of Baudelaire. There is, inherent in poetry, an obligation to turn unsatisfaction into a permanent object. In a first impulse poetry destroys the objects which it seizes. By destroying them it returns them to the elusive fluidity of the poet's existence and it is at this point that it hopes to regain the identity of the world and man. But at the same time as it releases the objects, it tries to seize this release. All it can do is to substitute the release for what it has seized from reduced life: it can never allow the release to take the place of the objects it once seized.

Here we are confronted with a difficulty similar to that of the child who is free to deny the adult, but who cannot do so without becoming an adult in his turn, and thereby forfeiting his freedom. But Baudelaire, who never assumed the prerogatives of the masters, and whose liberty guaranteed his insatiability to the end, nevertheless had to rival these beings whom he had refused to replace. Admittedly he searched for himself, never lost or forgot himself, and watched himself watching. The recuperation of being was, as Sartre indicated, the object of his genius, his tension and his poetic impotence. There can be no doubt that at the origin of the poet's destiny there is a certainty of uniqueness, of election, without which the task of reducing the world to oneself or of losing oneself in the world would lose its significance. Sartre makes this Baudelaire's defect. He attributes it to the isolation in which he was left by his mother's second marriage. This is indeed the "feeling of solitude since my childhood," "or an eternally solitary destiny" of which the poet himself spoke. But Baudelaire undoubtedly gave just as valid a revelation of himself when he said: "As a child I felt in my heart two contradictory feelings, the horror of life and the ecstasy of life."

We cannot sufficiently emphasise the certainty of irreplaceable uniqueness which is at the basis not only of poetic genius (Blake saw this as the common denominator which made poets similar to all men), but of every religion (of each Church) and of every country. It is quite true that poetry has always corresponded to the desire to recuperate, to mould in a tangible, external form a unique existence which was first unformed and which would otherwise only have been palpable within something, within an individual or a group. But it is doubtful whether our awareness of existing does not necessarily have that deceptive quality of uniqueness: the individual may feel it by belonging to a city, a family or even a couple (according to Sartre, Baudelaire experienced this as a child, bound body and heart to his mother), or he may feel it on his own account. Nowadays, no doubt, it is this latter case which brings about poetic vocations and which leads to a form of verbal creativity in which the poem is the recuperation of the individual. We could thus say that the poet is the part taking itself for the whole, the individual behaving like the community.

So states of unsatisfaction, objects which deceive or which reveal an absence, are the only forms through which the individual recovers his deceptive uniqueness. The city might fix it or establish it, but isolated existence alone has the chance to do what the city must and can do, without the power to do it. It is all very well for Sartre to say of Baudelaire: "his dearest wish was to *be* like the stone, the statue, in the repose of immutability." He can represent the poet as eager to extract some petrifiable image from the mists of the past, but the images which he left participated in a life which was open, infinite in Baudelaire's sense of the word, that is to say, unsatisfied. It is therefore misleading to maintain that Baudelaire wanted the impossible statue or that he could not exist, unless we immediately add that he wanted the impossible far more than he wanted the statue.

It would be more reasonable—and less contemptuous—to examine in this light the feeling of uniqueness or of awareness which Baudelaire had as a child, believing that he alone was the ecstasy and the horror of life and that nothing would alleviate its weight. We must examine all the consequences of "this miserable life." Sartre is justified in claiming that Baudelaire *wanted* something which seems ruinous to us. At least he wanted it as one wants the *impossible*—that is to say both genuinely as such, and deceptively, in the form of a chimera. Hence his tortured existence as a dandy, longing for work but bitterly engulfed in a useless idleness. But since, as Sartre admits, he was armed with "incomparable tension," he drew all he could from an untenable position. A perfect expression of ecstasy and horror gave his poetry a Fullness sustained *to the very limits* of a free sensibility, an exhaustive form of rarefaction and sterility which makes Sartre uneasy. The atmosphere of vice, rejection and hatred correspond to the tension of the will which denied the constraint of Good in the same way as the athlete denies the weight of the dumb-bell. It is true that every effort is fruitless. The poems in which this expression is petrified and which reduce existence to being, have made of *infinite* vice, hatred and liberty those tranquil, docile and immutable forms with which we are acquainted. It is also true that poetry which survives is always the opposite of poetry for, having the perishable as its subject, it transforms it into something eternal. But it matters little if poetry, whose essential nature is to unite the object of the poem with the subject, unites it with the poet, disappointed, unsatisfied and humiliated by failure. The object, the world, irreducible and unsubordinated, incarnated in the hybrid creation of poetry and betrayed by the poem, is not betrayed by the poet's unlivable life. Only the poet's interminable agony can really reveal the authenticity of poetry, and Sartre, whatever he may say, helps us to see that Baudelaire's end, preceding the glory which alone could have changed him to stone, corresponded to his will: *Baudelaire wanted the impossible until the end.*

BAUDELAIRE AND THE STATUE OF THE IMPOSSIBLE

A little discernment in the awareness of our own reality justifies hesitation. We cannot know "distinctly" what had supreme value for Baudelaire. Perhaps we should deduce some indication of the fatal relationship between man and value from the very fact that he chose to ignore it. We may betray what has supreme value for us if we have the weakness to decide about it "distinctly." There is nothing surprising in liberty demanding a leap, a sudden and unforeseeable snatch, no longer accorded to those who decide in advance. It is true that Baudelaire remained a maze for himself. Leaving every possibility open in every direction until the end, he aspired to the immutability of stone, the onanism of a funereal poem. We cannot help perceiving a permanence of the past within him, an exhaustion heralding inertia, a precocious old age, impotence. In *Les Fleurs du Mal* we find grounds for justifying Sartre's interpretation according to which Baudelaire made sure that he was only an "unchangeable and imperfectible" past and chose "to consider his life from the standpoint of death, as if a premature end had already fixed it."

The fullness of his poetry may be connected with the immobilised image of the trapped animal which he gave of himself, which obsessed him, which he continually evoked, just as a nation resolves to live up to the image it once had of itself and agrees to disappear rather than to fail it. Creativity which receives its limitations from the past comes to a halt. Because it has a feeling of unsatisfaction, it cannot detach itself and is content to live in a state of permanent unsatisfaction. This morose pleasure, prolonged by failure, this terror of being satisfied, changes liberty into its opposite. But Sartre stresses the fact that Baudelaire's life was played out in a few years and that, after the outburst of youth, it slowed down to an interminable decline. He writes:

> By 1846, [that is to say when Baudelaire was twenty-five] he had spent half his fortune, written most of his poems, given a definitive form to his relationship with his parents, contracted the venereal disease which was slowly going to kill him. He had met the woman who was to weigh like lead on every hour of his life, and he had accomplished the journey which was to furnish his work with exotic images.

But this view leads us to Sartre's opinion of the *écrits intimes*. They are repetitions, and they distress him. I would like to dwell on a letter dated January 28, 1854. In it Baudelaire gives the outline of a play. In a deserted spot at night a drunken workman meets the woman who has abandoned him. She refuses to return home with him, despite his pleas. In despair he leads her along a footpath, knowing that she will fall into a well. The episode originates with a song. "It begins," he wrote, "by:

> Rien n'est aussi-z-aimable
> Franfru-Cancru-Lon-La-Lahira
> Rien n'est aussi-z-aimable
> Que le scieur de long.

. . . Finally, this amiable sawyer throws his wife into the water. He then addresses a Siren . . .

> Chante Sirène Chante
> Franfru-Cancru-Lon-La-Lahira
> Chante Sirène Chante
> T'as raison de chanter.

> Car t'as la mer à boire,
> Franfru-Cancru-Lon-La-Lahira
> Car t'as la mer à boire,
> Et ma mie à manger!

The sawyer is burdened with the author's sins; by way of a change of key—a masque—the image of the poet suddenly thaws. It is deformed and changes. It ceases to be the image determined by a rigid rhythm, so tense that it moulds things in advance. The limited past no longer casts a spell. An unlimited possibility reveals the attraction which pertains to it—the attraction of liberty, of the rejection of limitation. It was not purely by chance that the theme of the sawyer and the idea of violating a dead woman were connected in Baudelaire's mind. At this point murder, lust, tenderness and laughter merge (he wanted to show the worker violating his wife's corpse on the stage).

"To see tragic natures founder," wrote Nietzsche, "and *to be able to laugh about it* despite the profound understanding, emotion and sympathy one may feel for them, is truly divine." So inhuman a feeling may well be inaccessible. In order to accede to it Baudelaire resorted to the feeble device of his hero's decline and the coarseness of his language. But nothing can touch the *peak* that Baudelaire reached with the *Siren*. We can see this from *Les Fleurs du Mal*, which he surpassed in this case. *Les Fleurs du Mal* ensured him a fullness of meaning and he pointed out their accomplishment. Baudelaire never completed his plan to write this play. His laziness or his impotence may have been the reasons. Or did the theatre manager to whom he suggested it inform him of the public's probable reactions? At least, in this outline, Baudelaire went as far as he could. From *Les Fleurs du Mal* to madness it was not the impossible statue but the statue of the impossible of which he dreamed.

THE HISTORICAL SIGNIFICANCE OF *LES FLEURS DU MAL*

The sense—or the non-sense—of Baudelaire's life, the perseverance of that instinct which led him from the poetry of unsatisfaction to the absence contained in total collapse, are not outlined solely in a song. A consistent and *determined* failure, which Sartre attributes to an erroneous choice, proves Baudelaire's horror at the idea of satisfaction. It proves his rejection of the constraints required by material profit. Baudelaire's position was as definite as it could be. In a letter to his mother he expressed a refusal to submit himself to the law of his own will. He wrote:

> Finally, it has been *proved* to me this week that I really can earn money—with a little application and perseverance I can earn a

great deal of money. But past misfortunes, incessant unhappiness, new debts to pay, the diminution of energy on account of minor annoyances, and finally my tendency to dream have put an end to everything.

We can regard this as an individual characteristic and, as such, as a form of impotence. We can also imagine things in time. We can judge that disgust with work so obviously connected with poetry as if it were an event which corresponded to an objective requirement. We know that Baudelaire submitted himself to this rejection, this aversion, after a deliberate decision and that even Baudelaire had, on various occasions, committed himself unremittingly to the principle of work. "At every moment," he wrote in his *Journaux intimes*, "we are crushed by the idea and the sensation of time. There are only two ways of escaping from this nightmare, of forgetting it: pleasure and work. Pleasure exhausts us. Work strengthens us. Let us choose." This attitude was similar to another, expressed a little earlier. "In every man, at every time, there are two simultaneous tendencies—one towards God, the other towards Satan. The invocation of God or spirituality is a desire to be promoted; that of Satan, or animality, is the joy of descending."

It is Baudelaire's first statement, however, which has the clearest consequences. Pleasure is the positive form of tangible life: we cannot experience it without an unproductive expenditure of our resources (it exhausts us). Work, on the other hand, is a form of activity. Its effect is the increase of our resources (it strengthens us). Now, "in every man, at every time, there are two simultaneous tendencies," one towards work (the increase of our resources), the other towards pleasure (the expenditure of our resources). Work corresponds to the care of tomorrow, pleasure to that of the present moment. Work is useful and satisfactory, pleasure useless, leaving a feeling of unsatisfaction. These considerations put economy at the basis of morality and at the basis of poetry. Always, at all times, the choice brings us to the vulgar and materialistic question: "Should I expend or increase my present resources?"

Baudelaire's reply was curious. On the one hand his notes are filled with the determination to work, but on the other, his life was a long rejection of productive activity. He even wrote: "To be a useful man has always seemed to me ghastly." The same impossible resolution of this opposition in favour of Good can be found on other levels. Not only did he choose God, as he chose work, in a completely nominal way, in order to belong to Satan more intimately, but he could not even decide whether the opposition was his own, within himself (between pleasure and work) or external (between God and the devil). All we can say is that he was inclined to reject its transcendental form. What in fact won the day with him was the refusal to work, to be satisfied by it. He only maintained the transcendence of obligation in order to accentuate the value of a rejection and to experience more forcefully the agonising attraction of an unsatisfactory life.

But this was not an individual error. The weakness of Sartre's analysis is exactly that he is content with this aspect. This is what reduces it to negative observations which have only to be situated in time or history for us to get a positive view. The collective relationship between production and expenditure is in history—Baudelaire's experience is in history. Positively, it has that precise sense which history confers upon it.

Like every activity, poetry can be regarded from an economic point of view. So can morality. Indeed, because of his life, and his unhappy reflections, Baudelaire placed the crucial problem in this domain. Sartre both broaches and avoids this question. He has made the mistake of representing poetry and the poet's moral attitude as the result of a choice. If we admit that the individual has made a choice, the sense of what he created is to be found, by others, in the needs which he has satisfied. The true sense of a poem by Baudelaire is not contained in his errors but in the historically determined expectation to which these errors corresponded. According to Sartre, choices similar to those made by Baudelaire appear to have been possible at other times. But they have never, before or since, had as their consequence poems similar to *Les Fleurs du Mal*. Sartre's critique does indeed contain some profound insights, although it neglects this fact. But it cannot account for the fullness with which Baudelaire's poetry has invaded the modern mind. Or, we might say, it only accounts for it inversely, inverted detraction turning unexpectedly to comprehension. Apart from an element of grace, or of luck, Baudelaire's "unparalleled tension" not only expressed individual necessity: it was also the result of a *material* tension imposed, historically, from without.

Insofar as it surpassed the individual instant, the society in which the poet wrote *Les Fleurs du Mal* corresponded to two simultaneous tendencies which are forever demanding a decision: society, like the individual, is forced to choose between care of the future and that of the present moment. Society is essentially based on the weakness of the individuals for which its own strength compensates. In a sense it is that which the individual is not—it is bound to the primacy of the future. Yet it cannot deny the present; that remains an element about which no definite decision is reached. This is where festivity comes in. During feasts, sacrifice constitutes the significant moment: it concentrates the attention on the expenditure of resources for the sake of the present moment—the expenditure of those very resources which care for the morrow should warn us to preserve.

But the society in which *Les Fleurs du Mal* was written was no longer that ambiguous society which sustained the primacy of the future and left the nominal presence of the present in a sacred form (disguised as a value of the future, a transcendental, eternal object, an immutable foundation of Good). It was capitalist society in full swing. It reserved as many of the products of work as possible for the increase of the means of production. This society was prepared to crush the luxury of the great even by terror. It turned away from a caste which had exploited the ambiguity of ancient society to its own advantage. It could not forgive it for having used for personal glory a part of the resources (of work) which could have been employed for the increase of the means of production.

Yet between the great lakes of Versailles and the dams of the industrial age, a decision was taken which was not merely in favour of the community opposed to privilege. The decision opposed the increase of productive forces for unproductive pleasure. In the middle of the nineteenth century, bourgeois society chose the dams: it introduced a radical alteration into the world. Between the day of Charles Baudelaire's birth and the moment of his death, Europe was covered by a network of railways. Production opened the prospect of an indefinite increase of productive forces and adopted that increase as its goal. The process which had been prepared some time earlier started a swift metamorphosis of the civilised world based on the primacy of the future—capitalist accumulation.

The proletariat had to oppose this process insofar as it was limited to the increase of the capitalists' personal profit: hence the workers' movements. The same process provoked the Romantic protest among writers because it put an end to the splendour of the *ancien régime* and replaced glory by utility. These two protests, therefore, though different in nature, were directed against the same object. The workers' movement, which was not opposed to the principle of accumulation, offered the liberation of man from the slavery of work as its goal. Romanticism, on the other hand, gave a concrete form to the prevention of man's reduction to utilitarian values. Traditional literature simply expressed the non-utilitarian values (military, religious, erotic) admitted by society or the ruling class, while Romanticism expressed the values denied by the modern State and bourgeois activity. But although it assumed a precise form, this type of expression was no less dubious. Romanticism was often limited to the exaltation of the past in an ingenuous opposition to the present. It was little more than a compromise: the values of the past had themselves come to terms with utilitarian principles. The theme of nature, which might seem to constitute a more radical form of opposition, merely offered the possibility of a provisional escape. Besides, love of nature can so easily be conciliated with the primacy of utility, that is to say of the future, that it has been the most common—and the most harmless—means of compensating for utilitarian societies. There is obviously nothing less dangerous, less subversive, or even less wild than the wildness of rocks.

At first sight the Romantic position of the *individual* is of greater consequence. To start with, the individual opposes social constraint by a dreamy, passionate existence which rebels against discipline. Yet the demands of the living individual are far from being consistent. They lack the hard and lasting coherence of a religious morality or of the code of honour of a certain caste. The only constant element among individuals is interest in increasing resources which the capitalist enterprises have the opportunity of satisfying. The individual is therefore the goal of bourgeois society just as hierarchy is the goal of feudal society.

Let us add that the pursuit of private interest is both the source and the end of capitalist activity. The great poetic form of individualism may seem excessive as a response, but nevertheless it is a response to utilitarian calculation. In its sacred form Romanticism was no more than an antibourgeois aspect of bourgeois individualism. Anguish, self-denial, nostalgia for the unobtainable expressed the unease of the bourgeoisie who, once they had entered history by committing themselves to the refusal of responsibility, expressed the opposite to what they were, but made sure that they never suffered the consequences of this opposite or benefited from them in any way. In literature, denial of the basis of capitalist activity only escaped belatedly from compromise. It was only at the peak of their activity and their development, after the sharp attack of Romantic fever, that the bourgeoisie felt at ease.

At this point literary research was no longer limited by a possibility of compromise. Baudelaire, it is true, had nothing radical about him—he always retained the desire not to have the impossible as his lot and to return to favour. But, as Sartre helps us to realise, he drew from his failure what others drew from rebellion. He had no willpower, but an instinct animated him in spite of himself. Charles Baudelaire's refusal was the most profound form of refusal, for it was in no way the assertion of an opposite principle. It only expressed that which was indefensible and impossible in the poet's obstructed state of mind.

Evil, which the poet does not so much perpetrate as he experiences its fascination, is indeed Evil since the will, which can only desire Good, has no part in it. Besides, it hardly matters whether it is Evil. If the contrary of will is fascination, if fascination is the destruction of the will, to condemn behaviour regulated by fascination on moral grounds may be the only way of really liberating it from the will. Religion, castes, and, more recently, Romanticism, had been a means of seduction. But then these very means of seduction began to use trickery, and obtained the approval of a will which was also prepared to use trickery. Poetry, therefore, which hoped to seduce the senses, had to limit its objects of seduction to those regulated by the will (conscious will which insists on such conditions as survival and satisfaction). Ancient poetry limited the liberty implicated in poetry. In the turgid mass of these waters Baudelaire opened a trough of cursed poetry which no longer assumed anything and which submitted itself to a fascination incapable of giving satisfaction, a fascination which was purely destructive. Thus poetry turned away from extrinsic requirements, from the requirements of the will, in order to satisfy one single intimate requirement which connected it with that which fascinated, which made it the opposite of will.

There is something other than the choice of a weak individual in this major determination of poetry. It hardly matters whether a personal inclination, involving responsibility, sheds any light on the circumstances of the poet's life. For us the significance of *Les Fleurs du Mal*, and therefore of Baudelaire, results from our interest in poetry. We would care nothing about an individual destiny were it not for the interest aroused by the poems. So we can only discuss it to the extent in which it is illustrated by our love for *Les Fleurs du Mal*—that is to say, not separately, but in connection with the whole. The poet's curious attitude towards morality accounts for the break which he effected: in Baudelaire the denial of Good was basically a denial of the primacy of the future. At the same time the assertion of Good contained an element of maturity (which regulated his attitude towards eroticism). It revealed to him both regularly and unfortunately (in a cursed way) the paradox of the instant to which we can only accede by fleeing from it and which eludes us if we try to seize it. There is no doubt that we can rise above Baudelaire's humiliating—and accursed—attitude, but even if we do so we cannot come to rest. We find the same humiliating misfortune in other, less passive, more reduced forms, which leave no subterfuge. So hard, or so extravagant, are they, that one might almost say that they constitute a savage happiness.

Baudelaire's poetry itself has been surpassed. The contradiction between a rejection of Good (of a value imposed by the will for survival) and the creation of a work which will survive, places poetry on that path of rapid decomposition where it was conceived, increasingly negatively, as a perfect silence of the will.

VICTOR BROMBERT

The Will to Ecstasy: The Example of Baudelaire's "La Chevelure"

L'ivresse est un nombre.

Two surprising lines, at the heart of this poem, alert us to the inadequacy of reading it literally, as a glorification of sensuous love.

> Je plongerai ma tête amoureuse d'ivresse
> Dans ce noir océan où l'autre est enfermé.
> (ll. 21–22)

These lines are no doubt suggestive of a physical experience, of what appears to be the central motif of the text. The verb *plonger* signals full immersion in the erotic-exotic imagery that can be traced back to the first stanza; the double enclosure ("dans," "enfermé") fuses the evocation of the lovers' alcove with the prestigious workings of synesthesia; the adjective "noir" qualifies the woman's hair, but also the bounded intimacy, and the descent into the secrets of the body which, by association, becomes the precious repository of memory. Yet things are not quite so simple. Two striking features of line 21 cannot be quickly dismissed. The first is the tense of the verb—"Je plongerai": a noteworthy use of the future in an evocative context stressing the past ("souvenirs dormant," "presque défunt"). The other, even more remarkable, is the metaphorical inversion "amoureuse d'ivresse" which reverses the expected order of priorities, making not of love but of intoxication the ultimate end. The adjectival form "amoureuse" in fact relegates love to a desiderative attribute.

From *Yale French Studies* 50 (1974). © 1974 by *Yale French Studies*.

It is the head ("ma tête") that counts: yet not the head of hair, but that of the poet's persona: the head that accomplishes the erotic movement, but also the seat of reverie and skilled perception. The expression "mon esprit subtil," two lines later, clearly supports such a reading. As for the metaphorical complexity of line 21, it serves to remind us that the true inebriation, announced by the exclamation "Extase!" in line 3, refers to the poetic sensibility, or more precisely to the poetic function itself.

That "La Chevelure" is in part about the poet should not come as a startling discovery. The pervasive use of the first person singular; the topos of the ecstasy-providing yet anonymous mistress; the imagery of quasi-death, resurrection and timelessness ("souvenirs dormant," "presque défunt"; "retrouver," "rendez"; "éternelle," "embaumé," "toujours") all give credence to such an interpretation. Moreover, the specific inebriation is linked to a figurative notion of drinking: it is the *soul* that wants to drink (line 16)—a notion that is delicately summed up in the concluding line, when the verb *humer*, applied not to a banal libation but to the very essence of memory, serves as an intermediary between the image of drinking and the more abstract one of breathing in. Any reader who recalls that in discussing the deep joys of wine, Baudelaire focusses immediately on the man who *drinks genius* ("l'homme qui boit du génie"), will of necessity make a further link between intoxication and the experience (or activity) of art.

The question is enriched by the ambivalent aesthetics of intoxication. The reference to Hoffman's *Kreisleriana*, at the beginning of *Les Paradis artificiels*, may seem trifling: Baudelaire recalls the advice given to the conscientious composer to drink champagne to compose a comic opera, Rhine wine for religious music, and Burgundy for heroic strains. This light-hearted reference in the opening section does serve a purpose: it provides a framework within which the notion of inebriation is explicitly placed in the service of art. The "qualités musicales des vins," illustrative of the system of synesthesia and foreshadowing the decadent "orgue à bouche" of Huysmans's hero Des Esseintes, are further related to temporal and spatial expansion, to the dynamics of escape. (The prose poem "Enivrez-vous" specifically recommends drunkenness as a way to avoid the martyrdom of Time!) Conversely, it is not surprising that music is directly evocative of the tormenting and delicious elation of artificial paradises: Wagner's *Tannhäuser* provides Baudelaire with the "vertiginous concepts of opium."

The relationship *art-ivresse* is further complicated by the dialectics of will and passivity: while the intoxications by drugs and art clearly imply a liberation, a "trip" (in the sense of a transport, or the literal meaning of *ecstasy*), is it not at all clear whether this signifies a weakening or, on the contrary, a concentration of the volitional powers. The dilemma is, of course, crucial to the poetic activity as understood by Baudelaire. On the one hand, any form of intoxication represents excess: it involves (the metaphor once again points to the aesthetic experience) "le développement poétique excessif de l'homme." The cost is always an extraordinary expenditure, a self-destructive "dépense de fluide nerveux." It marks a falling-off, a loss of the most precious substance: will.

On the other hand, not only some intoxicants (wine, for instance) "exalt willpower," but poetry specifically requires the "assiduous exercise of will and the permanent nobility of intention."

One has heard a great deal about Baudelaire's interest in drugs. It might be worthwhile, for a change, to look not at what the poet says about inebriation, but at how inebriation is by him related to the problems of poetry. What justifies such a perspective is a threefold dialectical tension in *Les Paradis artificiels* paralleling, at the level of the discussion about wine and hashish, the fundamental opposites of the creative method: egocentricity and depersonalization, passivity and control, intoxication as self-possession and artistic self-possession as inebriation.

First, depersonalization. The subtitle of "Du Vin et du hachish" refers to intoxicants as "moyens de multiplication de l'individualité": multiplication, but also dispersal, evanescence. A few pages later, Baudelaire asseverates that certain drinks possess the virtue of increasing ("augmenter") the personality enormously; they create, so to speak, "a third person." After a while, the personality disappears altogether (twice Baudelaire uses the formula "la personnalité disparaît"), and this vanishing act is brought into revealing juxtaposition with the poetic act, namely that of the "poètes panthéistes." Ultimately it is the generic "enthusiasm" of all poets and creators which is metaphorically illustrated by the painful delights of intoxication. I have attempted elsewhere to show how the lyric mode exists for Baudelaire in terms of a structured depersonalization: the poem functions as a specular system allowing for the subject to disappear in the object. In section 7 of "Du Vin et du hachish," the "great poets" are indeed seen as exercising their will to achieve a state in which they are simultaneously "cause et effet, sujet et objet."

Multiplication is a key word. Baudelaire likes crowds because they provide him with the dizzying "jouissance de la multiplication du nombre." Inversely, concerning the multiplication within the individual: "L'ivresse est un nombre." But this form of numerical, demultiplying, centrifugal intoxication seems contradicted by an intoxicating effect (or metaphoric use of intoxication) that stresses the self as the center of the universe. *Les Paradis*

artificiels insist on this opposing centripetal, and even solipsistic, trend. Hashish "develops excessively the human personality"; drugs in general encourage
"solitary pleasures," they "exaggerate" the individual, they wed him to himself. "Epouvantable mariage de l'homme avec lui-même!" Eventually, this
movement carries the individual to believe in his own godhead. He becomes
the monomaniacal center of his own cosmos. *"Je suis devenu Dieu!"*

If, in the dialectics of intoxication, egocentricity and depersonalization
remain interlocked, so do the opposing notions of passivity and control. This
too is directly relevant to the poetic activity. The rubric of passivity under
induced ecstasy is of course telling: will is lessened ("amoindrie"); the subject
becomes unfit for action ("incapable de travail et d'énergie dans l'action");
time disappears; the mind suffers from inexorable "évaporation." The very
measure of temporality is abolished. Yet the rubric of control is no less
impressive. The drugged subject retains the power to observe himself ("la
faculté de vous observer vous-même"); some forms of inebriation actually
"exalt will." More important, the "trip" toward the unknown appears in fact
as a volitive act: "Vous l'avez voulu. . . ." The absolutist aim is implicit:
"Les yeux visent l'infini." If the addict stares into his own Narcissus face,
it is not only out of self-gratification, but because of the workings of a
measureless proud will. In the last analysis, control itself induces a sense of
drunkenness. The "free exercise of the will," apanage of the genuine poet,
imposes the dreamer—somnambulist as his own magnetizer. In such power
lies joy. The *absolute* lyric mode implies an "absolute divinization" of the
poet; this joy involves a tension between enthusiasm and the analytic spirit.
In this tension, in this "état mixte," Baudelaire sees the essence of "modern"
poetry. These lyric dissonances, in turn, make of irony the pivot of the
modern poetic experience. And irony, in a contextual image that yokes the
active and the passive, is defined as the vengeance of the vanquished—"cette
vengeance du vaincu."

In "La Chevelure," this particular ironic tension is operative throughout.
More specifically, the dialectics of passivity and desideration, summed up
by the inverted metaphor "amoureuse d'ivresse" function as early as the first
stanza.

> O toison, moutonnant jusque sur l'encolure!
> O boucles! O parfum chargé de nonchaloir!
> Extase! Pour peupler ce soir l'alcôve obscure
> Des souvenirs dormant dans cette chevelure,
> Je la veux agiter dans l'air comme un mouchoir!

The poem opens with the vocative "O," repeated twice in the second line.
This triple exclamation imposes the ecstatic mode (here suggesting at first

adoration); it prepares indeed the word "extase" which, verbless and accompanied by only an exclamation mark, appears at the beginning of the third line much like a fourth vocative interjection. The passivity (or implied submissiveness) of the ecstatic mood is further stressed by the rather rare word "nonchaloir" denoting indolence, and the reference to the "sleeping" memories.

Yet the first stanza simultaneously proposes a clear volitive strand. The first signal comes in the third line; the intentional preposition "Pour," followed by the infinitive "peupler" (the verb itself suggests an active multiplication, and more specifically, procreation or even creation), announces the unambiguous volitional statement of the first stanza's closing line: "Je la veux agiter. . . ." These signals of intentionality, implying movement as well as a project, are further intensified by semantic elements suggestive of departure: "moutonnant" refers to the hair, but by indirection also to the waves of the sea; this double image is further developed or modulated by the preposition of spatiality "jusque," the adjective "chargé" (implying the load or *cargo* of a vessel), the waving of the handkerchief associated with leave-taking and—perhaps most important—the very first substantive of the poem, "toison" (fleece), referring to the hair, but immediately also, by means of the allusion to the mythological fleece, to the notion of an exotic voyage, of a quest.

These dual strands of passivity and intentionality become part of a larger network in the rest of the poem. The ecstatic and indolent strains of the opening stanza are echoed by the opening note of the next stanza (the adjective "langoureuse"), picked up by the nonactive "presque défunt" of line 7, continued by the more ambiguous "voguent" of line 9, and brought to a full suggestion of passivity by the "infinis bercements" and the "féconde paresse" of the fifth stanza. On the other hand, the semantic field is equally rich in volitional elements. "J'irai là-bas": the decisive future of line 11, applied to the elsewhere, obviously echoes the "Je la veux . . ." of the first stanza. This desiderative note is further strengthened by the imperative in line 13 ("soyez"), related in turn to the verb of movement "enlève" (though this verb also implies the passivity of the passenger). The beginning of stanza 5 repeats the attack of stanza 3: "Je plongerai"—another future of intentionality, itself echoed by the "Saura" of line 24, as well as by the verb "retrouver" denoting a search. In the last stanza, the sense of an intentional projection becomes explicit by means of the conjunction of purpose "Afin que . . ." and the subjunctive compounded by a categorically imperative negation "tu ne sois jamais. . . ."

The dual strands of the poem, though in steady transformation, remain in a state of tension until the end. This tension is in large part made secure by one of Baudelaire's key images, the port, here revealingly located at the precise center of the text. The port, place of refuge and reverie, is also the place of departure—or more precisely, the place of the reverie about departure. Ideal Baudelairean locus of controlled dreams, of a dandyish equilibrium between movement and stability, the haven ("séjour charmant," as he puts it in the well-known prose poem) opens up while it locks in. Not surprisingly, this central fourth stanza is also the one most heavily laden with quasi-religious images: "âme," "or," "vastes," "gloire," "ciel pur," "éternelle chaleur."

"La Chevelure" is not the only poem associating sea images with the apparently conflicting experiences of inebriating indolence and artistic control. "Le Beau navire" overtly describes the bewitchment of the "molle enchanteresse," as she lazily glides by ("Suivant un rythme doux et paresseux et lent"), and majestically displays her body rich with precious intoxicants.

> Armoire à doux secrets, pleine de bonnes choses,
> De vins, de parfums, de liqueurs. . . .

Yet the bewitching experience is, from the start, held in check by the opening volitive structure: "Je veux te raconter," repeated word by word at the beginning of the fourth stanza, and twice echoed within the two stanzas by the slight variation of the third line: "Je veux te peindre. . . ." Desire itself seems to be kept at a distance, the spell exorcised and held under control by these volitional structures and incantatory repetitions. The variation is equally revealing: the substitution of the verb "peindre" for the verb "raconter" clearly places the sensuous experience under the metaphoric supervision and discipline of art.

Such a framework of explicit artistic control appears as a recurrent pattern in the work of Baudelaire. The opening piece of *Tableaux parisiens*, which must be read as a sort of introduction, provides another telling example. The first line affirms the artistic intention:

> Je veux, pour composer chastement mes églogues. . . .

This is strengthened by the future construct of line 6 "Je verrai . . . " (repeated in line 13), the "Je fermerai" of line 15, the "je rêverai" of line 17, by the unequivocally intentional "Pour bâtir" of line 16, and brought to a logical conclusion through the glorification of artistic will:

> Car je serai plongé dans cette volupté
> D'évoquer le Printemps avec ma volonté. . . .
>
> (ll. 23–24)

Not only is the very notion of dreaming placed under the patronage of a future "creative" tense (I shall dream, I shall decide when and how to dream, I shall shape and dominate my dreams), but "volupté" represents here emphatically not that which art describes: it proposes itself as the very definition of *artistic will*. The analysis of this inversion, which in its own terms parallels the metaphoric structure "amoureuse d'ivresse," casts light on the concluding remarks of "Le Poème du haschisch" which glorify the "permanent nobility of intention" in the context of an essay devoted to the allurements and dangers of intoxication.

Baudelaire's ambivalent fascination with inebriating experiences, reenacted in "La Chevelure," is translatable into synonymous or metonymic images. There are indeed other words for this attraction, which is also a fear. Baudelaire himself, in referring to the phenomenon of evaporation associated with drug addiction, speaks of a "transposition": the pipesmoking is experienced as a smoking of oneself. But evaporation, in association with a sensuous spell, is precisely the devil's aim in his subversion of human will.

> Et le riche métal de notre volonté
> Est tout vaporisé par ce savant chimiste.

Baudelaire's work is colored by this fear, but also by the project to bring into a balanced, creative juxtaposition, the passive delights of ecstasy and the prerogatives of the individual's self-control. Ultimately, *will* itself—especially the artistic will—is conceived as a type of intoxication. "L'inspiration vient toujours quand l'homme le *veut*." However, it is a problematical intoxication, as the end of the sentence implies: ". . . mais elle ne s'en va pas toujours quand il veut." Only two sentences earlier Baudelaire speaks of those supernatural moments when time and space are boundlessly extended; and a sentence later he refers to the "sorcellerie évocatoire"—thus clearly suggesting that it is the very function of poetry to live out this tension between intoxication as experience and intoxication as method.

RITTER LIBRARY
BALDWIN-WALLACE COLLEGE

BARBARA JOHNSON

Poetry and Its Double:
Two "Invitations au voyage"

POETIC COOKERY

Mange-t-on dans René?
—BALZAC, *Falthurne*

On mange beaucoup dans les romans de Flaubert.
—JEAN-PIERRE RICHARD,
Littérature et Sensation

The prose version of Baudelaire's "Invitation au voyage" appeared in 1857, two years after its well-known homonym in verse. It did not, however, meet with the same success; already transported by the rhythmic precision and calm lyricism of the versified text, readers of the prose poem have always tended to decline its invitation. Their refusal, varying from regrets to indignation, generally takes the form of a comparison, devaluing the prose in favor of the verse. For example, the "Invitation" in prose, writes Jacques Crépet, "sounds infinitely less pure and less musical: it is weighed down by moral and practical considerations which drag it either toward the exposition of ideas or toward everyday reality." And Suzanne Bernard, after juxtaposing the verse poem's refrain—

> Là, tout n'est qu'ordre et beauté,
> Luxe, calme et volupté—

> [There, all is but order and beauty,
> Luxury, calm, and sensual pleasure.]

From *The Critical Difference: Essays in the Contemporary Rhetoric of Reading.* © 1980 by the Johns Hopkins University Press.

with the prose description of a "pays de Cocagne,"

> où le luxe a plaisir à se mirer dans l'ordre; où la vie est grasse et
> douce à respirer; d'où le désordre, la turbulence et l'imprévu sont
> exclus; où le bonheur est marié au silence; où la cuisine elle-même
> est poétique, grasse et excitante à la fois . . . ,

> [where luxury is pleased to mirror itself in order; where life is
> rich and sweet to breathe; where disorder, turmoil, and the un-
> foreseen are excluded; where happiness is married to silence;
> where the cooking itself is poetic, rich and stimulating at
> once . . . ,]

exclaims, "What! all *that* was in Baudelaire's dream of voluptuous beauty!
A quiet, comfortable life with 'rich and stimulating' food!"

In the act of refusing the invitation into prose, these readers thus accept
with a vengeance Baudelaire's invitation to compare. And their verdict is
generally the same: what is wrong with the prose lies in what it adds to the
imagery of the verse. The new elements are considered discordant, extra-
neous, and unpoetic. For the readers, then, every plus in the prose poem is
a minus.

For a small minority of readers, on the other hand, it is the very heterogeneity of the prose poem's imagery which heightens its poetic effect: "In
the 'Invitation au voyage' . . . seduction and tenderness reach their peak in
metaphors which unite abstract feelings with the most prosaic objects of the
culinary arts."

But however radical the divergence between these two ways of judging
the prose poem, their agreement over the element, namely, cooking, to
valorize or to condemn is striking. Considered either as a lapse in taste or
as a new stylistic spice, the unexpected presence of these culinary images
within a "poetic" text has always given rise to the same question, Can cooking really be poetic? This, however, is precisely the question the text does
not allow us to ask, since it has already answered: Cooking itself is poetic.
Rather than the status of the word *cooking*, it is the status of the word *poetic*
that is at stake. What must be asked is thus not Can cooking be poetic? but
What does *poetic* mean? Because the prose version of Baudelaire's "Invitation
au voyage" gives an affirmative answer to the first question, it renews the
urgency and uncertainty of the second.

If the text's own use of the word *poetic* in a culinary context is rejected
by certain readers, it can only be in function of a conception of poetry derived
from somewhere else. In Suzanne Bernard's case, this conception comes
from certain statements made by Baudelaire in his article on Banville:

> The lyre gladly flees all the details on which the novel feasts.
> The lyric soul strides as wide as a synthesis; the mind of the
> novelist regales itself with analysis.

For Bernard, then, *poetic* = *lyric*, and lyric poetry is no place for the kitchen. Baudelaire's distinction between the lyrical and the novelistic parallels the distinction suggested by our two epigraphs between the "lyrical" prose of Chateaubriand and the "realistic" prose of Flaubert: the presence or absence of the act of eating in the two works illustrates the Baudelairean distinction between the presence or absence of "detail"; "eating" in a text thereby takes on the status of an index to the text's genre.

Bernard's inability to swallow the "rich, stimulating food" in the prose "Invitation" thus results not from a simple excess of detail but from a conflict of codes. Cooking, which is certainly foreign to the lyric tradition, here disturbs the coherence of the poetic code—but it does so in order to reveal that the "poetic" is itself nothing but a code. Baudelaire indeed investigates the way poetry functions *as* a code in the prose "Invitation," as well as in many other prose poems. The fact that many readers find the genre of the *Petits poèmes en prose* problematic is due to what might be called a "code struggle" going on both between the verse and the prose poems and within the individual prose poems themselves.

If the mention of cooking in the prose "Invitation" thus represents the intrusion of a novelistic or realistic code in a poetic context—and we still of course do not know what "poetic" means—what is it that, within this so-called code struggle, can be said to represent the "lyric" code? Let us take another look at Baudelaire's distinction.

> The lyre gladly flees all the details on which the novel feasts.
> The lyric soul strides as wide as a synthesis; the mind of the
> novelist regales itself with analysis.

Curiously enough, the close relation between novels, details, and food is suggested here not only in the meaning of Baudelaire's statement, but also in its very terms, in the figurative use of the verbs *feast* and *regale* ("se régaler," "se délecter") to describe the work of the novelist. And while the verbs associated with novels thus evoke a kind of metabolic incorporation, the verbs associated with lyricism are rather verbs of hyperbolic motion (*flee, stride*): the delights of dining give way, in the lyric, to the pleasures of traveling. The lyric, in other words, turns out to be nothing other than a kind of *voyage*.

THE RHETORICAL VOYAGE

*Il n'y a rien qu'on puisse appeler langage avant l'articulation, c'est-à-dire la
différence locale. . . . La société, la langue, l'histoire, l'articulation . . .
naissent . . . en même temps que la prohibition de l'inceste.*
—DERRIDA, *De la grammatologie*

It is clear that a major participant in the prose "Invitation" 's code
struggle will be the text of the "Invitation" in verse, the lyric voyage par
excellence in Baudelaire's work. Let us therefore begin by analyzing the
nature of the lyrical invitation presented in that poem:

> Mon enfant, ma soeur,
> Songe à la douceur
> D'aller là-bas vivre ensemble!
> Aimer à loisir,
> Aimer et mourir
> Au pays qui te ressemble!

[My child, my sister, / Dream of the sweetness / Of going there
to live together! / To love at leisure / To love and die / In the
land that resembles you!]

In inviting his lady to the "land that resembles" her, the poem's speaker
begins not with a description of the land but with an affirmation of its
metaphorical status. What is being proposed to the woman is a place created
in her own image, a place toward which she would stand in necessary and
symmetrical relation, a place, in other words, that would serve as her mirror.
And indeed, the word *mirror* does appear in the very center of the poem.
The lyric voyage, then, is a voyage through the looking-glass, a voyage into
the illusory "depths" ("les miroirs *profonds*" [emphasis mine here and passim])
of a reflection. Its desired end is the perfect metaphorical union of the
destinatrice with the *destination*.

Grammatically, however, this seemingly transparent metaphorical spec-
ularity is not so simple. In speaking of the relation between the lady and
the land as a relation of perfectly symmetrical duality, we have not taken
into account the dialogical status of the metaphorical affirmation. But it is
precisely at the point at which the speaker seems to describe the metaphor
in terms of the most objectively referential, visual resemblance between lady
and land that its mediation through a third focal point becomes explicit:

> Les soleils mouillés
> De ces ciels brouillés
> *Pour mon esprit ont les charmes*
> Si mystérieux
> De tes traîtres yeux
> Brillant à travers leurs larmes.

[The watery suns / In these misty skies / *For my spirit have the very charm* / Which is so mysterious / Of your treacherous eyes / Shining through their tears.]

The important common denominator between land and lady, between suns and eyes, is less their shared shining roundness than a common effect produced on the "spirit" of the beholder. The rhetorical meeting point between the two terms (eyes and suns) is not simply that of a metaphorical resemblance but that of a metonymical third term, contiguous to both: the speaker's desire. Metaphor, in other words, is the effect, not the cause, of the metonymy of desire.

There is yet another problem in the seemingly transparent, referential grounding of the metaphor. For if metaphor consists, as Fontanier puts it, "in presenting one idea under the sign of another idea which is more striking or better known," what is it that here stands as the "better known" point of comparison, if not, paradoxically, a woman whose charms are mysterious and whose eyes are treacherous—a woman, in other words, who is quite unknown, and perhaps unknowable? The "you" that serves as the point of reference ("the land that resembles you") is itself the unknown in the equation. And the land where "all is but order and beauty, luxury, calm, and sensual pleasure" is not in reality a land that is just like the lady, but a description of what the speaker wishes the lady were like.

It is thus metaphor itself that has become an "Invitation to the Voyage," a process of seduction. And if, as the abbé du Bos puts it, poetry can be called "l'art d'émouvoir les hommes et de les amener où l'on veut" ("the art of moving men and leading them wherever one likes"), then this metaphorical seduction, this poetic voyage, does not consist of moving in space but of moving the desires of a person.

Let us examine the nature of this rhetorical operation more closely. In the opening invocation, "Mon enfant, ma soeur," familiarity coincides with familiality; the desired union between two contiguous beings ("vivre ensemble") is placed under the natural sign of genetic resemblance. The metonymic meeting between two separate subjects takes place within a metaphorical bond of biological likeness. And if such a union is by definition incestuous, then incest becomes, in rhetorical terms, the perfect convergence of metaphor and metonymy.

The same convergence can in fact be seen in the relation between the lady and the land; while a person's relation to place is by definition metonymic, that is, arbitrary and contingent, here it is said to be metaphorical, that is, motivated and symmetrical. Metaphor thus becomes a process both of writing—the writing of resemblance—and of erasing—the erasing of difference. And the difference it erases is not only that between person and place; it is nothing less than the difference between metaphor and metonymy as such. If the entire field of language is described as the space engendered by the two axes of metaphor and metonymy—that is, by their separation— the rhetoric of Baudelaire's "Invitation au voyage" would thus seem to be situated entirely at the intersection of the two axes, at the point which, in mathematical parlance, is called the *origin*.

Interestingly enough, the poem leads us toward this "origin" of language:

> Tout y parlerait
> A l'âme en secret
> Sa douce *langue natale*.

[There, all would speak / To the soul in secret / Its sweet *native language*.]

This evocation of a first, original language makes of the voyage not a departure but a return, the erasing of the distance covered by a previous voyage, the elimination of the interval that separates the "soul" from its origin. Again, we rejoin Baudelaire's remarks about lyricism: "Any lyric poet, by his very nature, inevitably brings about a return toward the lost Eden." Origin, Eden, incest: through the process of obliteration of all difference—spatial, temporal, linguistic, or intersubjective—the voyage seems to tend toward a primal fullness, immobile and undifferentiated, prior to movement, time, and law. This Edenic state of perfection indeed constitutes itself through the exclusion of imperfection, as its privative grammar indicates: "Tout *n'est que*. . . ." Each one of the abstract nouns following the "All is but . . ." seems to name—all by itself—the totality of "all"; paradoxically, the "all" is not equal to the sum of its parts; rather, it is the elimination of all partition.

Ultimately, however, this suppression of all difference, division, or distance can only result in a tautology without syntax, that is, in the abolition of language as an articulated space structured by differences. And just as the origin of a mathematical graph is the point at which all variables are equal to zero, this elimination of all variation or difference in language, this Edenic point of primal fullness, can only be a u-topia, a dimensionless point, a nonplace. The poetic "native language," the origin of signification, the convergence of metaphor and metonymy, in reality marks nothing less than the disappearance of language as such.

How then can we situate the language of this text with respect to the silence that is its origin and end? How does the text *say* the end of the voyage if the end of the voyage is an absence of text? Let us look at the poem's last stanza:

> Vois sur ces canaux
> Dormir ces vaisseaux
> Dont l'humeur est vagabonde;
> C'est pour assouvir
> Ton moindre désir
> Qu'ils viennent du bout du monde.
> —Les soleils couchants
> Revêtent les champs,
> Les canaux, la ville entière,
> D'hyacinthe et d'or;
> Le monde s'endort
> Dans une chaude lumière.

[See on these canals / These ships sleeping / In vagabond spirit / It is to fulfill / Your least desire / That they come from the ends of the earth. / —The setting suns / Clothe the fields, / The canals, the entire town, / In hyacinth and gold; / The world falls asleep / In a warm light.]

Are these ships, which "come from the ends of the earth" to "fulfill your least desire," in the process of leaving or arriving? In spite of the demonstratives ("*ces* canaux," "*ces* vaisseaux") and the present tenses ("ils viennent," "le monde s'endort"), the trip's end-point seems curiously missing. More curiously still, this eclipse of the end is inscribed as such in the text, by the use of a dash ("—Les soleils couchants"), which both opens up and deletes, within the very space of language, the locus of the end—of ecstasy or death. Indeed, the silence of the end is in no way an end; it is but a stroke of the pen, deferring for a moment what follows. If the poem's language is thus organized around its own disappearance, that disappearance turns out to be not an asymptotic limit external to the text—its end or origin—but its own necessary and inherent discontinuity, the very principle of its spacing, its articulation, and its rhythm.

DECLINING THE INVITATION

> *Cette fois, on sent l'effort dans ce système allégorique—qui remplace*
> *le tableau lumineux et calme évoqué à la fin du poème en vers.*
> —SUZANNE BERNARD,
> *Le Poème en prose de*
> *Baudelaire à nos jours.*

As we have just seen, the lyrical invitation operates on two levels which are traditionally called *rhetorical:* the level of *persuasion* (seduction) and the level of *figure* (convergence of metaphor and metonymy). In both cases, the poem tends toward the transformation of all plurality and difference into unity and sameness. In contrast, the rhetoric of the prose "Invitation au voyage" is, from its very first sentence, quite different:

> Il est un pays superbe, un pays de Cocagne, dit-on, que je rêve
> de visiter avec une vieille amie.

> [There is a superb country, a land of Cockaigne, they say, which
> I dream of visiting with an old friend.]

Contrary to the incestuous intimacy and shared dream of the verse poem, the prose poem begins not only without invocation but also without inter-locution. The lady is not at first addressed directly by the text, but is inscribed within the text in the third person ("une vieille amie"): she has become, in Benveniste's terms, not a person but a non-person, a grammatical instance designating her absence instead of her presence. This grammatical change in the invitation—which is thus no longer a real invitation—subverts the intimacy between "I" and "you" which, in the verse poem, had led to an Edenic "us" ("notre chambre") in which each could find in the other, trans-formed into the same, the essence of his own soul. Between the "I" and the "old friend," no direct seduction can take place: speaking *to* has become speaking *of*. The lady is depersonalized into a mere social role, the role of the "old friend," or, later, of the "chosen sister" ("soeur d'élection")—an expression that unmasks the entirely arbitrary, conventional character of the lyric invocation "my child, my sister." As a social stereotype, the lady in the prose poem changes from the unique object of an incestuous love to the locus of an infinite possibility of substitution.

In the same way, the usage of the third person subverts the originality and uniqueness of the speaker himself. The dream is announced from the very beginning as belonging to the language of others: "Il est un pays superbe, un pays de Cocagne, dit-on. . . ." The real author of this dream is not "I" but "they"; the dreamer dreams by hearsay, as part of the repertoire of social rites to which the sending of any invitation—or even any love poem—ultimately belongs.

Having thus begun by subverting the immediacy of the dialogue between the first and second persons by the constant intrusion of the third, the prose poem nevertheless goes on to make abundant use of the first and second person pronouns, which had in fact never appeared as grammatical subjects in the verse poem. Interlocution, which was absent from the opening lines of the prose poem, returns with a vengeance. It would thus seem that in conserving the I / you dialogue within a context that questions its very conditions of possibility, the prose poem is situating *its* dialogue not between the first and second persons, but between the function of person (*je, tu*) and the function of non-person (*elle, on*), between the lyric illusion of dialogic reciprocity and symmetry and the ironic asymmetry that disrupts and displaces that illusion.

While the prose poem thus puts in question the specular symmetry between the "I" and the "you," it nonetheless seems to accentuate and elaborate on the specular symmetry between the land and the lady:

> Un vrai pays de Cocagne . . . où tout vous ressemble. . . . Il est
> une contrée qui te ressemble. . . . Fleur incomparable, tulipe
> retrouvée, allégorique dahlia . . . ne serais-tu pas encadrée dans
> ton analogie, et ne pourrais-tu pas te mirer, pour parler comme
> les mystiques, dans ta propre *correspondance?* . . . Vivrons-nous
> jamais, passerons-nous jamais dans ce tableau qu'a peint mon
> esprit, ce tableau qui te ressemble? . . . Ces trésors, ces meubles,
> ce luxe, cet ordre, ces parfums, ces fleurs miraculeuses, c'est toi.
> C'est encore toi, ces grands fleuves et ces canaux tranquilles. . . .
> (Emphasis in original)

> [A veritable land of Cockaigne . . . where everything resembles
> you. . . . There is a land which resembles you. . . . Incomparable
> flower, rediscovered tulip, allegorical dahlia . . . wouldn't you
> be framed by your analogy, and couldn't you, to speak like the
> mystics, mirror yourself in your own *correspondence?* . . . Shall
> we ever live, shall we ever pass into this picture my mind has

painted, this painting that resembles you? . . . These treasures, these furnishings, this luxury, this order, these perfumes, these miraculous flowers, are all you. So are these rivers and tranquil canals. . . .]

The notion of "correspondences" mentioned in the poem embodies a conception of metaphor which was in fact an artistic commonplace in Baudelaire's day. From Swedenborg to Madame de Staël, from Schelling to the abbé Constant, the idea of correspondences served not only to account for "analogies among the different elements of physical nature" but also to reveal "the supreme law of creation, the variety in unity and the unity in variety." In other words, metaphor was a proof of the existence of God:

> All things in nature from the smallest to the largest are but so many correspondences, for the natural world exists and conserves itself through the spiritual world, and both of them through the Lord.

In Baudelaire's prose poem, the planting of the "flower" in a land comparable to it, the land of its "own correspondence," seems designed to insure both the stability of the flower's identity (its likeness to itself) and the unity and order of the whole poetic universe. If this flower is said to be, paradoxically, an *"incomparable* flower," if it is defined, in other words, as at once incomparable and comparable, being both what founds and what transcends the poem's system of comparisons, then the flower is indeed, like God, what can be likened to everything without ceasing to be unique. Metaphor here turns out to be a process of obliteration of the inherent contradiction between substitution (the comparable) and the unique (the incomparable).

Baudelaire, however, refers to the notion of correspondences not only so as "to speak like the mystics" but also so as to speak like—and comment on—another Baudelaire, the Baudelaire who wrote a sonnet called "Correspondances." In that sonnet, the word *comme* (like)—used seven times in fourteen lines—acts as a kind of "Archimedes' fulcrum" to lift up the "ténébreuse et profonde unité" ("deep, dark unity") of the world. Now, in our prose poem, the word *comme* occurs ten times, reaching an apotheosis in the following lines:

> Un vrai pays de Cocagne, te dis-je, où tout est riche, propre et luisant, *comme* une belle conscience, *comme* une magnifique batterie de cuisine, *comme* une splendide orfèvrerie, *comme* une bijouterie bariolée!

[A veritable land of Cockaigne, I tell you, where all is rich, clean and shiny, *like* a clear conscience, *like* a magnificent set of cookware, *like* the splendid wares of a goldsmith, *like* a gaudy set of jewelry!]

But here, instead of conveying a "deep, dark unity," the word *comme*— bringing with it, as we have seen, a code struggle, a conflict of codes— conveys a nonunified, heterogeneous plurality. In pushing *ad absurdum* the possibility of comparison, the prose poem transforms the word *like* from a necessary link in the world's order to a mere linguistic reflex, conventional and arbitrary. This ironic proliferation of likenesses does not render comparison impossible, but it does put in question the validity of taking comparison as a sign of the ultimate unity of the world.

In the same way, the lady to whom "all" is compared has become such a miscellaneous collection of objects ("treasures," "furniture," "luxury," "perfumes," "rivers," "canals") that she is finally nothing but that to which *anything* can be compared: this "allegorical flower" is no longer the point of primal convergence, of metaphorical fusion, where metaphor and metonymy, signified and signifier, harmoniously unite, but the very locus of substitution and of dissemination, a mere linguistic constant in an infinitely extensible equation.

Just as this allegorical flower has been rhetorically emptied of any reliable identity through the mechanical proliferation of its likenesses, so too the lyrical "soul"—central to the verse poem's inner voyage ("tout y parlerait / A l'âme en secret / Sa douce langue natale")—here undergoes a parallel transformation. In affirming that "tu les conduis [mes pensées] doucement vers la mer qui est l'Infini, *tout en réfléchissant les profondeurs du ciel dans la limpidité de ta belle âme*" ("you lead my thoughts gently toward the sea which is the Infinite, while *reflecting the depths of the heavens in the limpidity of your beautiful soul*"), the poet has transformed the very "depths" of the soul into a mere specular illusion. The correspondence between heaven and earth has literally become a play of reflections, not between two depths or essences, but between two shining surfaces. The image of the shining surface is in fact ubiquitous in this poem:

Les miroirs, les métaux, les étoffes, l'orfèvrerie et la faience y jouent pour les yeux une symphonie muette. . . . Un vrai pays de Cocagne, te dis-je, où *tout est riche, propre et luisant*, comme une belle conscience, comme une magnifique batterie de cuisine, comme une splendide orfèvrerie, comme une bijouterie bariolée!

[The mirrors, the metals, the cloth, the gold, and the crockery
play for the eyes a mute symphony. . . .]

"Everything" in this imaginary land thus resembles a glistening mirror—
including the "conscience" (consciousness, or conscience). Ironically, the
"belle conscience" has here become, in a literal sense, what it is often called
in a figurative sense: the seat of reflection.

But if everything has become a mirror, then the normal function of the
mirror as a confirmation of identity has been uncannily subverted and infinitely *mise en abyme*. In the very terms in which he invites the lady to the
land of her own correspondence and offers her an infinite reflection of herself,
the poet in fact transforms that self into an empty hall of mirrors: if the lady
can mirror herself in what resembles her ("ne pourrais-tu pas *te mirer* . . .
dans ta propre correspondance?"), she is no longer seen *in* the mirror; she
has become a mirror herself. And if the lady's "*propre* correspondance" (her
"*own* correspondence") is simply a surface that is "*propre*" ("clean"), then the
propriétés (properties) that are supposed to constitute identity are derived
from mere *propreté* (cleanness). The two senses of the word *propre* have
curiously become interchangeable.

But questions of property and propriety do not stop here. For if the
conscience is as clean as a set of pots and pans, then it must itself be part
of a general and daily housecleaning, in which dishwashing and brainwashing
are somehow equivalent. This brings us to the strange presence of moral
and economic considerations in the text of the prose "Invitation."

ETHICS, ECONOMICS, AND POETICS

*Je veux parler de l'hérésie de l'enseignement, laquelle comprend comme
corollaires inévitables l'hérésie de la passion, de la vérité et de la morale.
. . . La poésie ne peut pas, sous peine de mort ou de défaillance, s'assimiler à
la science ou à la morale; elle n'a pas la Vérité pour objet, elle n'a qu'Elle-
même.*

—BAUDELAIRE, *Notes nouvelles sur Edgar Poe*

"Il est une contrée qui te ressemble, où tout est beau, riche, tranquille
et *honnête*" ("There is a country which resembles you, where all is beautiful,
rich, tranquil, and *honest*"). Appearing as it does in the midst of an echo of
the verse poem's refrain, the word *honest* is doubly jolting: it breaks the
repetition, and it introduces into the prose poem a system of moral values
totally foreign to the voluptuous amorality of the verse poem. Like cooking,
honesty is the sign of the intrusion of a different code; it belongs to the

literature of bourgeois morality against which Baudelaire often vituperated, and which seems to assert, as Baudelaire puts it, that "any honest man who knows how to please his wife is a sublime poet." About Emile Augier's play *Gabrielle*, which received a prize for its morality, Baudelaire sneers:

> Listen to Gabrielle, virtuous Gabrielle, calculating with her virtuous husband how many years of virtuous avarice—with interest—it will take them to reach an income of ten or twenty thousand pounds. Five years, ten years . . . then, says this honest couple:
> WE CAN LIVE LIKE A WEALTHY PLAYBOY!
> . . . M. Augier . . . has spoken the language of shopkeepers . . . mistaking it for the language of virtue.

But curiously enough, the language of commerce and avarice is also the language of the prose "Invitation":

> Un vrai pays de Cocagne, te dis-je, où tout est *riche*, propre et luisant, comme une *belle conscience*, comme une magnifique *batterie de cuisine*, comme une splendide *orfèvrerie*, comme une *bijouterie bariolée!* Les *trésors* du monde y affluent, comme dans la maison d'un homme *laborieux* et qui a *bien mérité* du monde entier.
> . . . Ces énormes navires . . . tout chargés de *richesses* . . . ce sont mes pensées. . . . Tu les conduis doucement vers la mer qui est l'Infini . . . et quand, fatigués par la houle et *gorgés des produits de l'Orient*, ils rentrent au port natal, ce sont encore mes pensées *enrichies* qui reviennent de l'Infini vers toi.

> [A veritable land of Cockaigne, I tell you, where all is *rich*, clean, and shiny, like a *clear conscience*, like a magnificent *set of cookware*, like the splendid *wares of a goldsmith*, like a gaudy *set of jewelry!* The *treasures* of the earth abound there as in the house of a *laborious* man to whom the whole world is *indebted*. . . . These enormous ships . . . loaded with *riches* . . . are my thoughts. . . . You lead them gently toward the sea which is the Infinite . . . and when, fatigued by the swell and *stuffed with products from the Orient*, they come back to their native port, they are still my thoughts, grown *richer*, which come back from the Infinite to you.]

This trip to the Orient seems more like a business affair than an affair of the heart. What is sought in this voyage is not love, but "riches." Honesty exists only to protect property; everything becomes a commodity, including the "clear conscience," as useful to the "laborious man" as his pots and pans. The land of Cockaigne is no longer a land of erotic fantasy, but an exploitable source of riches, a colony.

This unexpected appearance of "shopkeeper language" in a text of poetic imagination thus forces us to examine three fundamental notions that underlie the bourgeois system with which the prose poem allies itself: the notion of value, the notion of work, and the notion of economy.

In the verse poem, the word *luxury* seemed to refer to some vague poetic quality called "Oriental splendor," having nothing to do with questions of production or exchange. But the source of the "treasures," which "abound" in the prosaic land of Cockaigne, is explicitly located in the working man's labor: "les trésors du monde y affluent, *comme dans la maison d'un homme laborieux* et qui a bien *mérité* du monde entier." If the imaginary country's value ("richesse," "luxe," "trésors," etc.) here results from a correspondence ("mérite") between work and wages, then the aesthetic notion of correspondences takes on an *economic* meaning.

This similarity between poetics and economics reaches a climax at the end of the prose poem, where the ships ("my thoughts") go out "loaded with riches" and come back "stuffed with Oriental goods." What the sonnet "Correspondances" calls the "transports of spirit and sense" are here literalized, making the metaphorical voyage (etymologically, *metaphor* literally means "transport") into a business trip. The prose poem thus reveals that "poeticity" has its own economy, that the equating of signifier with signified, of the lady with the land, functions in the same way as the equating of wage with labor, or of product with price.

It is, however, precisely in *opposition* to the economy of exchange that the prose poem situates its ultimate object of desire:

> Qu'ils cherchent, qu'ils cherchent encore, qu'ils reculent sans cesse les limites de leur bonheur, ces alchimistes de l'horticulture! Qu'ils proposent des prix de soixante et de cent mille florins pour qui résoudra leurs ambitieux problèmes! Moi, j'ai trouvé ma *tulipe noire* et mon *dahlia bleu!* (Emphasis in original)

> [Let them search, let them go on searching, let them push back forever the limits of their happiness, these alchemists of horticulture! Let them offer to pay sixty or a hundred thousand florins to anyone who can solve their ambitious problems! As for me, I have found my *black tulip* and my *blue dahlia!*]

It is this priceless, "incomparable" flower that, representing the highest poetic value, seems to locate the poetic universe somewhere beyond and above the economic sphere. This aesthetic transcendence of the structure of economic exchange is indeed a commonplace of traditional poetics:

> For a fine art must be free art in a double sense: i.e., not alone in a sense opposed to contract work, as not being a work the magnitude of which may be estimated, exacted, or paid for according to a definite standard, but free also in the sense that, while the mind, no doubt, occupies itself, still it does so without ulterior regard to any other end, and yet with a feeling of satisfaction and stimulation (independent of reward).
>
> Whereas a unique content is required of prose, in poetry it is the unique form which is dominant and lasting. It is the sound, the rhythm, the physical relations among words . . . which predominates, at the expense of their capacity to be consumed as a definite, indisputable meaning.

The economy of the work of art is thus organized around a signifying surplus that transcends the mere exchange between signifiers and signifieds, between tenors and vehicles. This excess, which engenders poetic value, constitutes, with respect to the system of exchange of equivalents, both its other and its *raison d'être*. For the exchange system—which has by no means disappeared, since it serves as a negative point of comparison for the production of poetic value—no longer exists in the service of the *comparable* (the "definite, indisputable meaning"), but, paradoxically, now functions in the service of the *incomparable*, the flower of poetry "Itself". "Poetry," writes Baudelaire, "cannot, under pain of death or decay, be assimilated with science or morality; it does not have truth as its object, it has only Itself." This same idea perpetuates itself today in Jakobson's well-known definition of the poetic function: "The set (*Einstellung*) toward the MESSAGE as such, focus on the message for its own sake, is the POETIC function of language."

How can we understand this paradoxical relation between a system of metaphorical equivalence and the engendering of its own transcendence? Curiously, Marx describes in these same terms the relation between a system of direct exchange and the emergence of capitalism. Let us compare a number of parallel extracts from poetic and economic texts:

> MARX: A particular kind of commodity acquires the character of *universal equivalent*, because all other commodities make it the material in which they uniformly express their value.

BAUDELAIRE: . . . tout vous ressemble, mon cher ange, . . . Ces trésors, ces meubles, ce luxe, cet ordre, ces parfums, ces fleurs miraculeuses, *c'est toi.*

MARX: The commodity that figures as universal equivalent is . . . *excluded* from the relative value form. This equivalent *has no relative form of value in common* with other commodities.

BAUDELAIRE: Fleur *incomparable* . . .

MARX: The simple circulation of commodities—selling in order to buy—is a means of carrying out a purpose unconnected with circulation, namely, the appropriation of use-values, the satisfaction of wants. The circulation of money as capital is, on the contrary, *an end in itself.*

BAUDELAIRE: La poésie . . . n'a pas la Vérité pour objet, elle n'a qu'*Elle-même.*

MARX: The circulation of capital has therefore no *limits.*

BAUDELAIRE: Ces énormes navires . . . tout chargés de *richesses* . . . ce sont mes pensées. . . . Tu les conduis doucement vers la mer qui est *l'Infini.*

MARX: The exact form of this process is therefore M-C-M′ [money-commodity-money +], where $M' = M + \Delta M =$ the original sum advanced, plus an increment. This increment or excess over the original value I call "*surplus-value.*" The value originally advanced, therefore, not only remains intact while in circulation, but adds to itself a surplus-value or expands itself. It is this movement that converts it into capital. (Emphasis in original)

BAUDELAIRE: . . . là-bas, où les heures *plus* lentes contiennent *plus* de pensées, où les horloges sonnent le bonheur avec une *plus* profonde et *plus* significative solennité. . . . Ce sont mes pensées *enrichies* qui reviennent.

[There where the slower hours contain more thoughts, where the clocks toll happiness with a more profound and more significant solemnity.]

The message spelled out by this collage of quotations is certainly not simple, but it incontestably suggests a resemblance between Poetry and

Capital, through their common way of transcending a system of equivalences *in the very process of perpetuating it*. The circulation of language as poetry is strikingly similar to the circulation of money as capital, and the "poetic" could indeed be defined as *the surplus-value of language*.

In combining metaphors of commerce with a panegyric to the priceless, the prose poem thus succeeds both in thematizing the traditional opposition between the poetic and the economic and in subverting that very opposition by inscribing a capitalistic model behind the structure of poeticity. But if in the very act of proclaiming its opposition to and transcendence of the economy of exchange—which is taken as "economy" per se—poetry parallels the logic of capital, then poetry's blindness to its own resemblance with economic structures is hardly accidental. On the contrary, it would seem that this type of misapprehension and denial of its relation to other codes might be constitutive of poetry as such. In fact, it seems that the function of the prose poem is precisely to reveal what poetry is blind to about itself, not by in turn opposing the poetic as such, but by making its functioning more explicit.

THE SWEET NATIVE LANGUAGE

Telle est la puissance imaginaire des horticulteurs que, tout en regardant leur spéculation *comme manquée à l'avance, ils ne pensèrent plus . . . qu'à cette grande tulipe noire réputée chimérique comme le cygne noir d'Horace et comme le merle blanc de la tradition française.*
—ALEXANDRE DUMAS PÈRE, *La Tulipe noire*

Vous n'êtes rien, frêles beautés,
Au prix des rêves enchantés
Qui tourbillonnent dans sa tête.
Nulle part il ne voit complète
L'oeuvre de Dieu,
Il rêve le dahlia bleu.
—PIERRE DUPONT,
"Le Dahlia bleu"

In the economy of the prose "Invitation," the "you" with which all is equated, the "flower" at once incomparable and infinitely comparable, thus serves as the universal equivalent, and hence represents poetry, "Itself." It is doubtless not by chance that poetry should here be represented by a flower: the poetic entity to which this prose poem most directly refers is precisely a *Fleur du Mal*. Perhaps the true addressee of this poem is not a lady but a lyric: "L'Invitation au voyage" in verse. It is thus between two *texts* that the true dialogue of the prose poem situates itself.

But the textuality of this "allegorical flower" is not confined to its ref-

erence to a *Fleur du Mal*. For far from consisting simply of new or warmed-
over Baudelairean rhetoric, this incomparable flower is also designated by
the names of two other well-known literary works—Alexandre Dumas's *Black
Tulip* and Pierre Dupont's "Blue Dahlia"—both of which had become, in
Baudelaire's day, common clichés for an unattainable ideal. We thus find
ourselves confronted with a paradox: this exceptional, incomparable flower
("qu'ils cherchent . . . j'ai trouvé"), this uniquely personal possession ("*Moi*,
j'ai trouvé *ma* tulipe noire et *mon* dahlia bleu"), turns out to be, in truth, an
impersonal linguistic commonplace, a perfectly ordinary find. What could
be the function of this use of devalued language to express the highest poetic
value? What is the relation between the exceptional and the common, the
priceless and the devalued? In making of the incomparable a cliché, is Baudelaire not reversing his own system of poetic values? The use of these two
commonplaces in a context that seems to call rather for some strikingly novel
expression indeed runs counter to the cult of originality which has always
underlain romantic poetry. Even as fine a critic as Georges Blin finds himself
disconcerted by this flagrant descent to banality:

> There is an extraordinary gap between the banality of the con-
> temporary references (to a popular novel and a poem) and, on
> the other hand, the lyricism, in blue and black, that for us, a
> century later, constitutes their mystery. What was the author's
> intention?

But what the prose poem puts in question here is the very postulate of the
unity of the subject presupposed by this notion of "author's intention."
Italicized in the text, the *black tulip* and the *blue dahlia* designate not the
apotheosis of the quest, but the unsettling of the authority of the quester.
The typographical change is a change of voice, or rather an ungovernable
pluralization of the "sources" of language. What, indeed, is a cliché, but an
authorless quotation? The question is thus not, as Blin seems to phrase it,
Who is speaking here, the *je* or the *on?* but rather, Can the act of speaking
have *one* subject? Can the boundary line between *je* and *on* ever really be
determined?

The "sweet native language" postulated by the verse poem is thus no
longer the unique, primal language of a unique individual, but rather the
authorless language of commonplaces and borrowed discourse, through
which man is born into language not as a speaking subject, but as a *spoken*
subject.

In making explicit the process of stereotypization which underlies all
language as both the result and the source of poetic discourse, Baudelaire's

prose poem indeed predicts, in the same breath, its own valorization and its own devaluation:

> Un musicien a écrit l'*Invitation à la valse;* quel est celui qui composera l'*Invitation au voyage,* qu'on puisse offrir à la femme aimée à la soeur d'élection? (Emphasis in original)

> [A musician has written the *Invitation to the Waltz;* who will be the one to compose an *Invitation to the Voyage* that one can offer to the beloved woman, to the chosen sister?]

In citing its own title as a future offering to the beloved, the text here already refers to itself as a potential cliché, as a currency of seduction coined to participate in a stereotyped ritual of exchange. Through its own self-quotation, the "Invitation au voyage" reads itself, like the land of Cockaigne and the black tulip, as the linguistic property of *on*, not yet written but already part of historical repetition.

From the commonplace flower (black tulip, blue dahlia) to the commonplace land (the land of Cockaigne), from the "you" of the home port to the "you" of the exotic shore, the entire poetic voyage thus takes place within the familiar bounds of clichés: rhetorical displacement in effect never leaves the common place. This familiar commonplace (indeed, universally equivalent with *all*) is, however, at the same time strangely foreign; its appeal is that of an unfamiliar, "unknown land." But the "*nostalgia* for an *unknown* land" ("cette *nostalgie* du pays qu'on *ignore*") which motivates the voyage is not, paradoxically, an attraction to the absolutely new, but the fascination of an invitation to *return,* of a call to "come back":

> . . . de toutes choses, de tous les coins, des fissures des tiroirs et des plis des étoffes s'échappe un parfum singulier, un *revenez-y* de Sumatra, qui est comme l'âme de l'appartement.
>
> Un vrai pays de Cocagne, te dis-je . . . (Emphasis in original)

> [. . . from all things, from all corners, from the cracks in the drawers and from the folds in the fabrics springs a singular perfume, a *come back* from Sumatra, which is like the soul of the apartment.
>
> A veritable land of Cockaigne, I tell you . . .]

The invitation to return, whose source, as Baudelaire's italics indicate ("*revenez-y*"), is in another text—an Other text—marks the call of the familiar

as unfamiliar. The voyage to the land "which one could call the Orient of
the Occident" ("qu'on pourrait appeler l'Orient de l'Occident") here becomes
not the search for some faraway utopia, but the quest for what (dis)orients
all return and all repetition, a quest, in other words, for what subverts the
very *sense*—or direction—of the voyage. If u-topia (no-place) and the com-
mon-place are ultimately indistinguishable (as Dumas indeed suggests by
comparing his utopian black tulip to the "white crow of the French tradition"
and to the "black swan of Horace"), it can only be because the truly un-
reachable utopian place, the place which is par excellence unknowable, is
not some faraway mysterious land, but the very place where *one is*.

CORRECTION AND EXTENSION

*Ce qui était poème redevient prose, et les éléments inédits qui auraient dû
renouveler le sujet, paraissent surajoutés intellectuellement.*
—HENRI BRUGMANS, " 'L'Invitation au voyage' de Baudelaire"

In contrast to the lyrical "Invitation," which seeks to return to a "native"
language and a state of primal, natural integrity anterior to social, temporal,
and rhetorical differentiation, the prose poem, which reevaluates the devalued language of clichés, explicitly privileges artistic belatedness over natural firstness:

Pays singular, supérieur aux autres, *comme l'Art l'est à la Nature*,
où celle-ci est *réformée* par le rêve, où elle est *corrigée, embellie,
refondue.*

[A singular land, superior to the others, as *Art is superior to Nature*,
where Nature is *revised* by dream, where it is *corrected, embellished,
reworked.*]

It is tempting to consider this valorization of correction and revision as a
description of the prose poem's own status with respect to the verse poem,
which can easily be seen as the "Nature" that must be reformed, the "raw
material" or pre-text to which the prose poem's "Art" is applied. Indeed,
the importance of the process of revision and transformation is constantly
thematized in the prose poem through the ubiquitous use of verbs of transformation: *illustrer, bâtir, décorer, allonger, colorer, tamiser, ouvrager, diviser,
réformer, corriger, embellir, refondre, chercher, reculer, éloigner, peindre*, and even
cuisiner.

But how does the work of transformation manifest itself concretely in the textual relations between the two "Invitations"?

Compared with the spare verticality of the verse poem, the well-filled paragraphs of the prose poem have always led readers to consider the prose as an expanded version of the "same poetic idea," translated into a freer, more verbose style. According to J. B. Ratermanis, the prose poem is constructed "by the successive development of elements whose main points (and not more than that!) are provided by the verse poem; some of the associations they contain are simply made more explicit." For Suzanne Bernard, "all of what was merely suggested or implicit in the verse poem is now taken up again, detailed and circumstantiated in the prose." Whether these additions are then considered appropriate or foreign to the original idea, whether their presence is "jarring" or raises the text's "seduction" to its "peak," the governing principle behind the prose poem's elaboration remains the same: it consists of repeating, developing, expanding, and making explicit the contents of the verse poem.

This conception of the prose poem as the amplification of a repeated poetic kernel seems to be confirmed by the structure of the prose "Invitation"; through the repeated return of certain opening lines ("Il est un pays . . . un pays de Cocagne . . . un vrai pays de Cocagne. . . . C'est là qu'il faut . . . Oui, c'est là qu'il faut . . ." etc.), the text takes shape by repeating and expanding upon its own starting points. Whereas verse is constructed out of the repetition of ends (rhymes), prose here develops by repeating its beginnings. The absence of any a priori limits to the extensibility of prose means that its measure can be taken only after the fact; in order to have reached an end, prose is only capable of marking a new beginning. It is perhaps this rhythm of returns and prolongations that conveys the impression that the prose poem is an amplified repetition of the verse poem, its "starting point." This impression is also supported by Baudelaire's description of his *Petits poèmes en prose* as still being "*Fleurs du Mal*, but with *much more* freedom, more detail, and more raillery."

The common formula for the prose poem thus seems to read as follows: "It is still the same thing (as the verse), but with much more: prose = verse + X." However, should this formula be taken literally? Is the process of correction really mere addition, simple explicitation, pure secondary elaboration of the "same poetic idea"? What, in other words, is the status of what the prose poem is supposed to be repeating?

In order to investigate this question, let us compare the verse and prose versions of the "refrain":

Là, tout n'est qu'ordre et
   beauté,
Luxe, calme et volupté

Un vrai pays de Cocagne, où
tout est beau, riche, tranquille,
honnête; où le luxe a plaisir à se
mirer dans l'ordre; où la vie est
grasse et douce à respirer; d'où
le désordre, la turbulence et
l'imprévu sont exclus; où le
bonheur est marié au silence; où
la cuisine elle-même est
poétique, grasse et excitante à
la fois, où tout vous ressemble,
mon cher ange.

[There, all is but order and
beauty, / Luxury, calm, and
sensual pleasure.]

[A veritable land of Cockaigne,
where all is beautiful, rich,
tranquil, honest; where luxury
is pleased to mirror itself in
order; where life is rich and
sweet to breathe; where
disorder, turmoil, and the
unforeseen are excluded; where
happiness is married to silence;
where the cooking itself is
poetic, rich and stimulating at
once, where all resembles you,
my dear angel.]

We have already pointed out the dissonant effect produced by the sudden
appearance of the word *honest* in the prose version. However, this inclusion
of a bourgeois value in a poetic context is not a simple addition of a new
value to the existing ones, but rather, a transformation of the very notion of
value. The very dissonance between the positive values of aesthetics and
those of the ethics makes explicit the negativity—the purely differential
nature—of linguistic values. For while *tranquil* alone is more or less synonymous with the verse refrain's *calm*, this correspondence is suddenly broken by the contamination of the word *honest*. *Tranquillity* becomes
retrospectively different from itself, evoking not the quiet harmony of an
exotic landscape, but the safety of a proprietor secure in the civil order that
guarantees both his freedom and his property. In the same way, while *order*
and *luxury* had in the verse poem been separated by *beauty*, which gave them
an aesthetic coloring, their relation in the prose poem no longer has anything
aesthetic about it: luxury mirrors itself in the *law-and-order* of institutionalized
forces designed to protect and perpetuate it. And the word *sweet*, which in
the verse poem conveyed a delicate tenderness ("Songe à la *douceur*"), here
becomes a mere condiment, making life into a tasty consumer product ("la

vie est grasse et *douce* à respirer"). What is added to the lyric vocabulary is not simply foreign to it; in the transformation produced by these additions, it is the repeated elements which become somehow foreign to themselves. In this struggle between codes, it thus becomes impossible to determine where one code ends and another begins. And if, as the critics would have it, the prose poem repeats the "same theme" as the verse poem, it is in order to question both the idea of *same* and the idea of *theme*.

This differential work of supplementation, in which the "same" becomes the "other," is explicitly described in the poem:

> Pays singulier, noyé dans les brumes de notre Nord, et qu'on pourrait appeler l'Orient de l'Occident, la Chine de l'Europe, tant la chaude et capricieuse fantaisie s'y est donné carrière, tant elle l'a patiemment et opiniâtrement illustré de ses savantes et délicates végétations.

> [A singular land, drowned in the mists of our North, and which could be called the Orient of the Occident, the China of Europe, so freely has warm, capricious fantasy acted on it, patiently and stubbornly illustrating it with knowing and delicate vegetations.]

This rhetorical transformation of the Occident into the Orient by the illustration of fantasy can easily be seen as the very image of the prose poem's "explicitation" of its versified original. Indeed, is not this singular land, which could be called "the Other of the Same," precisely what poetry has become? For it is not prose that is here opposed to poetry, but poetry that, reworked by prose, has separated from itself—not by becoming what it is not, but by making manifest its status as a pure linguistic value, constituted by its own difference from itself.

CORRECTION AND CASTRATION

Nous pouvons couper où nous voulons . . .
—BAUDELAIRE, *Dédicace aux Petits poèmes en prose*

Our examination of the validity of the formula ("prose = verse + X") that underlies the traditional analysis of this text has brought us to the point at which it is no longer possible to distinguish the "same" ("verse") from the "other" ("X"). But even the most literal-minded attempt to divide the text of the prose poem into what is repeated and what is added soon reveals not

only that this distinction is inoperative, but that the text of the verse poem
has to a large extent materially disappeared. Let us compare, for example,
the following extracts:

D'aller là-bas vivre ensemble!
     Aimer à loisir
     Aimer et mourir
	C'est là qu'il faut aller vivre,
	 c'est là qu'il faut aller mourir.

[To go there to live together! / To love at leisure, / To love and die]	[It is there that one must go to live, it is there that one must go to die.]

In the verse poem, the words *live* and *die* are mediated by the repetition of
the word *love*, which gives them an erotic connotation. But in the prose, *live*
and *die* are juxtaposed without any *love:* the voyage could just as well be
solitary as amorous. This elimination of the word *love* from what is supposed
to be a love poem may seem surprising. But if we add up everything the
prose poem does *not* repeat, we find that "charmes," "tes yeux," "larmes,"
"beauté," "volupté," "chambre," "assouvir," and "désir" have been eliminated
along with "aimer" and "ensemble." What has disappeared in the passage
from verse to prose is the very process of seduction.

The text of the verse poem has thus not simply been mounted in prose
like a jewel in a new setting. Before being "repeated," the verse poem has
had its main erotic moments amputated. This process of amputation is at
work on a formal level as well: the transformation of verse into prose involves
a similar elimination of the moments of intensity (rhythm, rhyme) which
give poetry its seductive charm. It is not by chance that what the prose poem
cuts out of the lyric is its eroticism. For this textual amputation, this suppression of the lyric's semantic and formal potency, corresponds quite literally
to the moment of castration.

That castration is somehow constitutive of the prose poem is repeatedly
suggested throughout the various texts of Baudelaire's *Petits poèmes en prose*,
where metaphors of violent blows and cuts indeed proliferate. In "Perte
d'auréole" ("Loss of Halo"), in which Baudelaire specifically allegorizes the
passage from poetry to prose, the amputation of the poet's halo—the "in-
signia" of his poetic power—necessarily precedes his entry into the "mauvais
lieu" of mere prose. And the breaking up of versification itself is perhaps
dramatized in the "Mauvais Vitrier": the poet's gesture of smashing the panes
of glass can be read as a play on the pun "briser les verres" ("smashing
glass")="briser les vers" ("smashing verse"). The passage from poetry to
prose seems to involve an amputation of everything which, in poetry, is
erected as unity, totality, immortality, and potency.

EXCLUSION/INCLUSION: POETRY AND ITS DOUBLE

Aimer une femme, passe encore, mais une statue, quelle sottise!
—FLAUBERT, *La Tentation de Saint-Antoine*

But what is the true nature of this potent poetic unity and totality, which is denatured and mutilated by the prose? What does the integrity of the lyric code—the "before" of the moment of castration—in fact comprise? The lyric seems to answer:

> Là, tout n'est qu'ordre et beauté,
> Luxe, calme et volupté.

It is this harmonious "all," this image of indivisible totality, which becomes, in the prose,

> Un vrai pays de Cocagne, où tout est beau, riche, tranquille, honnête; où le luxe a plaisir à se mirer dans l'ordre; où la vie est grasse et douce à respirer; d'où le désordre, la turbulence et l'imprévu sont exclus; où le bonheur est marié au silence . . .

"All is but order and beauty"; "Where all is beautiful, rich, tranquil, honest": the evocation, in both cases, begins with the word *all*. And since it is precisely the notion of totality which is in question, since it is toward totality that poetry aspires—the subject's unity or the incestuous union in the perfect metaphorical return to the origin—an analysis of the function of the word *all* in the two texts may indeed turn out to be revealing.

We have already noted that, in the verse poem, this totality results not from infinite inclusiveness but rather from restrictive exclusiveness ("Tout *n'est que* . . ."). The list of abstractions which compose this totality ("ordre," "beauté," "luxe," "calme," "volupté") are superimposed upon each other like metaphorical mirrors of one unique poetic essence ("tout"). In the prose poem, on the other hand, the verb *être* is no longer limited a priori by a restrictive construction ("ne . . . que"), and, in the place of the paradigmatic series of equivalent abstractions, we find a syntagmatic list of descriptive adjectives and arbitrarily juxtaposed details subordinated to the adverb "où" ("where"). Thus consisting of an extensible collection of miscellaneous properties and fragmentary descriptions, the prosaic *all* is metonymic rather than metaphoric, inclusive rather than exclusive, circumstantial rather than essential. The passage from essence to attribute is a passage from totality to partition; while the poetic *all* is as such indivisible, the prose poem's *all* is divided into a series of attributes whose number can be indefinitely increased without being able to exhaust the meaning of *all*, the sum of which the enumeration indefinitely defers. In becoming, through its infinite extensibility, the conflictual locus of a struggle among heterogeneous and incompatible codes, the "tout est" of the prose does not thereby designate, however, another specific code that would as such be opposed to the poetic one ("realism," "prose," "ordinary language"); rather, the prose "tout est" allegorically represents the code of the non-totality of all codes. "All is," in other words, names not a totality but a *set*, a set of codes, that is, a set of sets. And just as modern set theory entails the fundamental paradox that "the set of all the sets in a universe is not a set," the "tout est" of the prose poem demonstrates that the code of all the codes in a semiological universe cannot, in turn, become a code.

Among the diverse attributes of the land of Cockaigne, the following is particularly significant: "le désordre, la turbulence et l'imprévu *sont exclus*" ("disorder, turmoil, and the unforeseen *are excluded*"). Could this exclusion of disorder not be read as an explicitation of the implicit exclusivity in the verse poem's "tout n'est qu'ordre"? If so, then the prosaic transformation of the poetic abstractions ("order," "beauty," "luxury," "calm," "pleasure") into a series of descriptive properties—properties that introduce into the prose poem economic and social codes foreign to the poetic code—is not simply a secondary elaboration: it is an explicitation of what the abstractions were originally abstracted from, of that from which the verse poem's refrain refrained. The poetic code is thus simply a set of elements considered "poetic" but also a process of exclusion and of negation, of active repression of whatever belongs to other codes. If, then, as Georges Blin puts it, Baudelaire's prose poems literally contain "*what is excluded* from *Les Fleurs du Mal*," their function is to make explicit not only *what* poetry excludes, but its very constitutive *act of excluding*.

That the act of excluding and cutting might in fact be constitutive of poetry as such is suggested not only by the "ne . . . que" syntax of the lyric "Invitation" but also by the insistence of exclusive formulations in Baudelaire's general remarks about poetry:

La Poésie . . . *n'a pas* d'autre but *qu'*Elle-même . . . elle *n'a pas* la Vérité pour objet, elle *n'a qu'*Elle-même.

[Poetry . . . has *no* end *other than* Itself . . . it does *not* have Truth as its object, it has *only* Itself.]

In viewing itself as the unmediated voice of the soul, as the original expression of subjectivity, poetry is blind both to its own status as a code, and to its relation to other codes, that is, to its own necessary mutilation produced by the very process of exclusion on which its sense of wholeness and uniqueness in fact depends. The forces of order which guard the poetic frontier are designed not only to repress, but to erase—wipe clean—the very traces of repression, the very traces of the cleaning operation. Only then can poetry—"propre et luisante comme une belle conscience"—seem to be "pure," that is, cut off from the process of its own production, from any history or context that is not Itself; cut off by what Jacques Derrida has called "a pure cut without negativity, a *without* without negativity and without meaning."

This obliteration and forgetting of the process of production and the consequent overestimation of the object produced, this erection of a fixed, statufied form as proof against mutilation and incompleteness, is characteristic of what both Marx and Freud have called fetishism. Both as a monument set up against the horror of castration and as a seemingly "mystical" product divorced from the work of its production, poetry—the potency and seemingly inexhaustible wealth of language—indeed reifies itself into a sort of linguistic fetish. Fixed in its "pure," immortal form, erected against the "movement that displaces lines" ("le mouvement qui déplace les lignes"), poetry, like Beauty in Baudelaire's well-known sonnet of that name, is nothing other than a "dream of stone" ("rêve de pierre"), the very image of death, castration, and repression which it is designed to block out and to occult.

If the prose poem thus consists of a textual act of subversion of the fetish, of the amputation of the lyric text, the verse poem in its turn, through its fundamental gesture of exclusion ("tout *n'est que* . . . "), was already constituted by a process of mutilation and occultation of another text, a heterogeneous cultural text strained by conflicts among codes—a text, indeed, that very much resembles the "Invitation au voyage" in prose.

Between the prose poem and the verse poem, in other words, the work of mutilation and correction operates indefinitely *in both directions*. Each of the two texts is the pre-text of the other; neither can claim priority over the other: the "raw material" is always already a mutilated text. This reciprocal correction is, however, not symmetrical: while it is the diverse heterogeneity of cultural codes which is excluded from the verse, the infinite inclusiveness of the prose extends as far as to include the very gesture of exclusion. But to include the exclusion of inclusiveness is to erase or put in question the very boundary between the inside and the outside, the very limits of poetic space. In doing so, the prose poem ultimately questions its own exteriority to poetry ("prose") as well as its interiority to it ("poem"). Internally external to the poetry it both repeats and estranges from itself, the prose poem becomes the place where castration and fetishization, valorization and de-valuation, repression and subversion, simultaneously oppose each other and undermine their very opposition. Neither poetry's "other" nor its "same," the prose poem thus constitutes nothing less than poetry's *double:* its double space as the space of its own division, as its "other stage" where what has been repressed by poetry interminably returns in the uncanny figures of its strange familiarity, where poetry, the linguistic fetish, the "dream of stone"—whether a *Commendatore*'s statue or an implacable Venus with marble eyes—suddenly begins to speak from out of the Other, from out of what is constituted by its very inability to determine its own limits.

GEORGES POULET

Exploding Poetry: Baudelaire

Who am I—I, Baudelaire? The answer to this question, constantly put forth by the poet, is always instantaneous and the same: I am a man, that is to say, a fallen being, ashamed of existing, doing evil, trampling in mud that is no different from me. Moreover, in my misery as in my baseness I discover that I am a poet. But a poet is no different in kind from other men; he is simply one in whom the repulsive traits common to all men are most clearly in evidence, thus inspiring from first glance a more vivid sense of horror. I, Baudelaire, because I am a poet, am eminently representative of human vileness. My situation is unexceptional, but the consciousness I have of it is in itself exceptional. Not for an instant do I forget the fact that my nature, like that of the entire human species, is one of degradation, and that the mud in which I trample fills a place essentially low and dark—a place into which the whole of creation, by reason of a Fall that occurred at its origin and irrevocably altered its essence, has forever slipped.

Consciousness of self in Baudelaire is of a complex character from the outset. It is the consciousness of a being who experiences in an extraordinary manner within himself a fate shared by all beings; and it is further a consciousness of that fate as the consequence of a change brought about at the very source of life. It is as if, the instant he was created, the first man and all of his descendants with him had undergone an incomprehensible mutation, such that, for the rest of the time allotted them on earth, men are condemned to be pulled in two opposite directions: conscious of being both

From *Exploding Poetry: Baudelaire/Rimbaud*, translated by Françoise Meltzer. © 1984 by the University of Chicago. University of Chicago Press, 1984.

the heirs of certain riches, possessors of a certain initial nature, yet dispossessed of that nature and dispossessed of that wealth.

At a certain point in his life, Baudelaire will link this dual and contradictory consciousness of self to a religious belief, that of original sin. His
religion, as Marcel Ruff has shown, is an aggravated Jansenism. For Baudelaire, as for the disciples of St. Augustine and Jansen, the natural depravity
of man is tied to the belief in an original Fall, which engendered the loss of
an initial state of happiness and glory. In contrast to the general denial of
original sin—a denial which, in Baudelaire's view, serves as a patent example
of the blindness of his age—for Baudelaire there is an opposing predication.
Yes, original sin exists: its influence alone can explain the duality found in
all men as soon as they examine themselves or look deeply within themselves.

This duality implies heights and depths. Theological space is a chasm.
The sinner is he who, because of the burden of his culpability, slides toward
and finally falls over the precipice. From that moment on, the only essential
relation for him is the one established between two points separated per-
pendicularly. The Baudelairean being, like the Hugo being, is essentially
one who lives the experience of the chasm into which he has plunged. For
the author of the *Flowers of Evil*, however, this descent into the abyss does
not have the same brutality as the Fall of the human (or angelic) being in
Hugo. For Hugo, the Fall is both crushing and without bounds. It is the
hideous substitution of the void for plenitude, a tragic manner of being lost
in the immensity of a cosmos replaced by its opposite, nothingness. Conversely, in Baudelaire, the descent of the damned occurs almost slowly. It
is never too rapid to be registered in some fashion from moment to moment
and place to place by the one who is subject to it. Thus the poet can measure
at a glance "the vertiginous staircase which engulfs his soul," and if the
damned descends "endless staircases without railing" in the dark, he follows
its spiral step by step:

> Hence, lamentable victims, get you hence!
> Hells yawn beneath, your road is straight and steep.

> *Descendez, descendez, lamentables victimes,*
> *Descendez le chemin de l'enfer éternel.*
> ("Delphine et Hippolyte," trans. Aldous Huxley)

It goes without saying that the space traveled does not have the rigidly
perpendicular quality of vertical space. Baudelaire's damned follows a sloping
surface that allows us to see him throughout his progression toward the
underworld. His movement from high to low and from good to evil is not

without transition. He succumbs, on the contrary, to the allurement of a gentle and yet irresistible incline. It is by degrees that he moves along the path of his destiny.

The following text is from a poem written by the young Baudelaire:

> There is a deep well, a symbolic Gehenna,
> Where Debauchery, that vile black queen, reigns.
> Within its walls, an endless staircase uncoils:
> The path taken here is never taken twice;
> Love plunges, strangled by the foul air.
> From step to step, down the spiral
> She will tumble, poor degraded soul,
> Down to those obscure depths, upon which no eye has gazed.

> *Il est un puits profond, symbolique Géhenne*
> *Où trône la Débauche, immonde et sombre reine.*
> *Un escalier sans fin tourne dans ses parois:*
> *Le chemin qu'on y fait ne se fait pas deux fois;*
> *L'amour tombe étouffé dans l'air qui s'en exhale.*
> *De degrés en degrés au bas de la spirale*
> *Elle ira descendant, pauvre être dégradé,*
> *Jusqu'au fond ténébreux que nul œil n'a sonde.*

Let us postpone examining the significance of these gloomy depths, though that is the most important of Baudelairean sites, and limit ourselves for now to the descending motion that spirals downward, thus leading the one who follows its meanderings from one extremity of existence to another. One is reminded here of the movement followed by the prisoner of Piranesi's "Carceri." The intinerary to which the Baudelairean damned conforms, leading into the dark expanses described by the poet, makes its way through an essentially Piranesian world. Yet Piranesi's name is never encountered in Baudelaire's work. No matter. It is of no great consequence whether or not the poet was directly influenced by the artist. He was certainly indirectly influenced. As was shown several years ago by Luzius Keller, the Piranesian view of the world left its mark on the greater part of French poetry in the nineteenth century. Nodier, Hugo, Nerval, Musset, Gautier—each, after his own fashion, transposed into verse the visions of Piranesian ruins and prisons. There are huge rooms, their visible dimensions further increased by a series of stairways, along which the same figure—the prisoner or the damned—disappears and reappears, following a path from landing to landing that will lead him to perdition. Baudelaire needed only to delve into the works of the previous or contemporary generation of poetry to find this obsessive vision. Moreover, he could not avoid encountering it at the heart of a work he admired almost above all others—a work he wished to translate and write a commentary upon because he sensed such similarities between the world it evoked and his own mental universe. Indeed, Thomas de Quincey's *Confessions of an Opium Eater* is nothing more than a prodigious rhetorical amplification of the theme of man as prisoner—prisoner of a movement ceaselessly repeated by his thoughts; a movement that seems, in this obsession, to follow an endless staircase that can lead him not to salvation but only to a hellish end. Nothing could be more immediately Baudelairean than this portrait of a wretched soul, less the captive of the walls enclosing him than of the steps he takes attempting to avoid his fate while in fact engulfing himself ever more deeply into its consummation. The Piranesian and Baudelairean worlds are similar. They are mutually illuminating, to the point that the latter seems to be the verbal commentary of the former. This world is essentially that of the abyss; not so much a space into which one falls and dies as an intermediate area between the high and the low, between light and absolute darkness, between hope and despair—a halfway point which, far from linking the extremes, marks the impossibility of establishing any connection between them.

A wholly mental space; a space of a vertigo which comes to light between two parts of the mind, to both of which the roads are blocked.

A space that can also appear in the form of an immense ceiling crowning the dark interior edifice and revealing the total absence of communication between the place from which one departed and that to which it leads:

> I seemed every night to descend—not metaphorically, but literally to descend—into chasms and sunless abysses, depths below depths, from which it seemed hopeless that I could ever reäscend.

It is indeed vain to hope for a climb back up to the daylight, for a screen blocks the light from the self, preventing light from triumphing over dark. "No eye from heaven can penetrate" the place into which the Baudelairean being sinks. An enormous lid extends everywhere above him. At times it appears as a veil, which the mind draws across the ideal place it dreams of, because it can no longer tolerate contemplating that place: "O ends of autumn . . . —my love and gratitude I give you, that have wrapped with mist my heart and brain as with a shroud, and shut them in a tomb of rain." A song of praise that in fact is a statement of despair. Passionately as the Baudelairean persona may at times wish to accept a fate that condemns him never again to climb back to the daylight, that separates him forever from his ideal and his joy—he cannot help seeing himself lying at the bottom of a tomb. The macabre quality of the tomb is not the principal reason for which Baudelaire chooses to remain in it. The burial vault is not solely a place of unfathomable sadness, "into which enters no rosy or gay beam of light"; it is even more the place outside of which, beyond reach, everything rosy and gay is to be found. Thus the Baudelairean being's sliding descent into the abyss has the result of creating a transcendence above the abyss. A transcendence whose presence, remote, inaccessible, and utterly foreign to that which it transcends, can conceive of itself only as the confirmation of an essential difference between the transcender and the transcended. Such are the "vanished coconuts of hidden Africa," of which the negress's hagard eye dreams, "behind the thickening granite of the mist." Thus the ceiling, the curtain, the veil, the lid assert themselves as a closure beyond which the happiness lost is to be found. At times the density is such that it creates something like negative depth, a distance at once spatial and temporal, too vast for the mind to hope ever to cross. This distance is the past; not the past lost and dreamed of, in the age before the Fall, but rather the past that has elapsed since the Fall, the evil past. It extends backward like the open country of an existence irrevocably polluted over its entire expanse. Nothing is more rigorously imagined by Baudelaire than this system of two pasts—one radiant and paradisiac, followed by another, dark and irreparable.

Baudelaire is the poet of irreparability, that is, of remorse:

> How shall we kill this old, this long Remorse
>   Which writhes continually
> And feeds on us as worms upon a corpse?

> *Pouvons-nous étouffer le vieux, le long Remords,*
>   *Qui vit, s'agite et se tortille,*
> *Et se nourrit de nous comme le ver des morts?*
>   ("L'Irréparable," trans. Sir John Squire)

The past to which remorse is connected is not the happy past, the one directly evoked by a nostalgic thought. What is rather remembered here is an indelible series of errors by reason of which, in the span of one lifetime, an individual has completed his downfall and forever parted with his portion of the inheritance. And the mnemonic image which for Baudelaire reigns immutable, at the gates of mental life is one of a decayed beauty, of a soiled happiness; flowers of evil, in the sense that the flower of good and happiness has disguised itself as its opposite. It is a memory of the senses, at times even of the flesh, for what is almost always preserved is an experience inscribed on the body as it is on the soul of whoever has been its subject. In any case, Baudelaire never ceases being haunted by his bad past, that sinister self-portrait which, like a curse or stigma, follows him throughout his life. "I am like a wearied man who looks back and can only see, in the depth of years, disillusionment and bitterness."

These "deep years" are often mentioned by Baudelaire. Depending upon the context, they designate affective worlds, each very different, which embrace extreme sadness as well as extreme joy. But in all of the numerous cases in which the poet measures this oscillation, the result for him is a characteristic dilation of the consciousness of self. For Baudelaire, existence manifests itself in the guise of an immense continuity, seen from a receding perspective in which an individual recognizes himself all the way along. I, Baudelaire, am not simply the moment I am presently living. I am a line that projects itself and, in so doing, is not obliterated along the path already traveled. Surely this is why Baudelaire attempts simultaneously to recall and to flee his past. One the one hand, he has no choice but to recall it, since to live is to become endlessly, retrospectively conscious of the transformation of the present into elapsed time. On the other hand, how horrible it is to discover that one cannot modify even the most insignificant of past events. More than anyone else, Baudelaire has a vivid sense of the process of immortalization by which all that slips into the past is paralyzed in it forever. The poet of remorse is then also the poet of irremediable time, time lacking in all freedom of being. It is a time that fossilizes as it passes from the present into the category of time elapsed. Consequently, in one form or another, whether as the damned descending the stairs without a bannister, whether as a ship trapped in polar icebergs, but always a slave to fate—Baudelaire offers himself as the victim of some diabolical Destiny, which, having assigned him an irrevocable lot, never tires of watching over him to ascertain that it is executed in all of its severity, with neither abatement nor mitigation.

Henceforth Baudelairean time will most often manifest itself in the form of a time fixed in advance and entirely contained in its previous segment. Neither the present nor the future can ever prevent the *stoppage* of time. Time is no longer a becoming; it is a continuing state. "There are eternal situations," says Baudelaire," and everything having to do with the irremediable falls into that category." Eternal situations are those in which the future and present cannot be distinguished from the past that determines them. Consequently there is in Baudelaire a perspective by which the depth of existence is merely the unfolding of an identical human landscape as far as the eye can see. One is reminded here of Mallarmé's swan, frozen forever in the same position, for the landscape reflects the same undefined, monotonous quality; it is a time trap from which all desire for escape is futile. It is no doubt to this particular type of lived time that Baudelaire alludes when, in a letter written to his mother in 1861, he tells her of the "continuity of horror" he glimpses before him. And it is assuredly with the same outlook in mind that Baudelaire—confronted several years earlier by the guardian who imposes upon him indefinitely the same restrictions and obligations—feels himself overcome by a nameless rage, complete with vomiting and vertigo. He writes: "I saw before me an endless series of years without family, without friends, without the friendship of a woman. . . ."

The irreparable is thus the interminable. It is the transformation of time into a sinister eternity, similar to the privative time span, frozen within itself, which is the punishment reserved for the damned. In the general universe of their existence, the damned have a single preoccupation: remembering their unalterable past. Such is remorse. It becomes the single element of thought, the exclusive object of the mind's activity.

Baudelairean time may also be viewed as a perpetuity, but of a special and particularly malevolent type; a destructive perpetuity. "My soul is prey to the Irreparable / It gnaws with tooth accurst." In one sense, time appears to be immobile, since it cannot be altered. In another sense, it reveals itself to be the incessant annihilator of everything it contains. The essential process suggested by the act of gnawing is one of an imperceptible but tireless destruction of being. Somewhere, Baudelaire writes: "Time eats life," and then adds immediately that this dark enemy "preys upon the heart." Elsewhere he says that man is "blind, and deaf, and like a wall unsteady / Where termites mine the plaster." Or, once again: "As the immense snows a stiffened body hide / So Time devours me momentarily."

Thus time is at once frail as an insect and vast as space. On the one hand it is reduced to the corrosive activity of a minute creature. On the other, it is magnified to the proportions of total space, where there is no longer time because there is no longer movement. This ultimate disappearance of time merging into the uniformity of space fires Baudelaire's imagination. He describes this moment as a gradual slowing down of things:

> I envy the least animals that run,
> Which can find respite in brute slumber drowned,
> So slowly is the skein of time unwound.

> *Je jalouse le sort des plus vils animaux*
> *Qui peuvent se plonger dans un sommeil stupide,*
> *Tant l'écheveau du temps lentement se dévide!*
> ("De profundis clamavi,"
> trans. Desmond Harmsworth)

The immobilization of time thus produces the same effect as the unification of space. The consequence of both is an intense feeling of ennui. Baudelaire's ennui resembles the tormenting deprivation of the individual, which is Pascal's ennui. It is not unlike the inertia or lethargy which lies in wait for the *homme sensible* of the eighteenth century. But it is also a very tangible notion: the persistence of a state rendered insufferable by dint of its invariability. Even more, it is the consciousness of this invariability, that is, of the irrevocable quality of fate. The result is that, on the one hand, the Baudelairean being recognizes the immutability of his lot with increasing intensity; on the other hand, he strains to repress his awareness of that lot—hence his desire to find refuge in a dreamless sleep. The ennui described by Baudelaire is thus a complex form of experience. It is a maximum of consciousness in a minimum of action; or, more precisely, it is a maximum of consciousness which has as both its cause and its effect a minimum of action. Seen from the perspective of this intensification of consciousness, and in the absence of all other activity, time becomes intolerably long:

> Nothing can equal those days for endlessness
> When in the winter's blizzardy caress
> Indifference expanding to Ennui
> Takes on the feel of Immortality.

> *Rien n'égale en longueur les boiteuses journées,*
> *Quand sous les lourds flocons des neigeuses années*
> *L'ennui, fruit de la morne incuriosité,*
> *Prend les proportions de l'immortalité.*
>   ("Spleen," trans. Anthony Hecht)

A feeling of heaviness is connected to time's length. The poet wants to find some occupation which will take "Time from his slothfulness, the world from spleen" ("et les instants moins *lourds*").

But all in vain! "Each moment, we are crushed by the thought and feeling of time." The result of a consciousness greatly heightened by time is not only further elongation, but greater heaviness as well. Time is essentially heavy. It makes itself felt through a paralyzing pressure; and if it is true that it activates the powers of the mind, it also concomitantly atrophies any creative power. After Vigny, Lamartine, and Nerval, before Mallarmé, Baudelaire is one of the French poets who has suffered the most from sterility: "I felt myself beset," he writes, "with a type of Gérard-like [Gérard de Nerval] illness, to know the fear of no longer being able to think or write a single line"—"the fear," he continues, "of seeing the admirable poetic faculty, the distinctness of ideas, and the power of hope which in truth make up my capital—of seeing them used up and endangered, and seeing them disappear in this hideous existence rife with shocks and jolts."

In short, impotence arises very early on in Baudelaire's life, "terrible, impassable, like the polar glaciers." This wholly negative feeling never leaves him, and always will tend to increase its sterilizing power. Thus monstrously, the dualism of the poet's spiritual life is furthered: he is simultaneously conscious of himself and conscious that this self of his does nothing, is nothing, and can only be an absence of being.

Hence the need in Baudelaire to restore a type of unity for himself by annihilating one of the opposing tendencies within him.

The desire to sleep forever is for him "a vile and disgusting wish, but a sincere one." "There are times when I suddenly want to sleep eternally." "I want to sleep! To sleep rather than live!" "Resign yourself my heart, poor beast, sleep sound."

This resignation, which is a renunciation, pushes him as far as to dream of suicide. One day when he is contemplating killing himself, he writes a very beautiful and very lengthy letter, the essence of which is that he is ending his life because he can no longer endure living, because "the fatigue of falling asleep and the fatigue of waking up are too much for him to bear."

Only an uninterrupted sleep would seem tolerable to him. But sleep is never entirely uninterrupted. Dreams emerge, giving away secret yearnings. And after dreams in sleep there are also daydreams. As Sartre has pointed out, Baudelaire always wants to be elsewhere; elsewhere than in his inertia, elsewhere than in his remorse, elsewhere than in the awareness of his degradation. To dream of being elsewhere is thus at the same time to dream of being other, to dream of having another self, another temperament, in a different place. Baudelaire's obsession with traveling is more than geographic in nature. His most fundamental desire is to achieve an eschatological displacement. We shall see this more clearly below, when we examine the means by which Baudelaire attempts to flee his essential condition—the state of being of a fallen nature. The dream of happiness which transports him to an imaginary India or Holland ideally transfers him to a place where it seems to him permissible to rediscover himself such as he was or was to have been before the Fall, in the state that theologians call "pure nature." Without for the moment pausing to examine these voyages whose destination is an allegorical country, let us nonetheless note that the Baudelairean voyage, including the mental one, lacks a destination as well as a time span; for "the true voyagers are those who move / simply to move." They go they know not where. And if, in the end, they choose death as their final destination, it is because it is not a concrete destination. It is not a determined or determinable *place*. It is simply an *over there*, as different as possible from the loathed *here:* "The first inn encountered"—"the place from which you will be absent."

In short, the essentially wandering character of Baudelairean thought is lacking in all finality, that is, in all well-defined ideality. This brand of thought attempts in no way to conform—as does Lamartine's, for example— to a preexisting model of an eternal idea, which anticipates the thought as a goal to be reached. Nothing could be less Platonic than Baudelairean thought. It does not project into the future a predetermined paradigm of beauty and happiness, which it then attempts to catch up with in order to conform to it. In fact, the more serious problem is that Baudelaire has the greatest difficulty in giving this future any positive aspect. If we exclude a few recurrent dreams, of which we will speak [elsewhere], we must conclude that Baudelaire proves himself incapable of a clear conceptualization of any future whatever. For him, the future is simply the possibility of extracting himself from the crushing burden of the present, and to clear at one bound the temporal conditions of existence. Thus the elsewhere and the future are above all centrifugal in function; a pure *beyond* (*au-delà*), characterized by the total absence of characteristics:

> Above the valleys and the lakes: beyond
> The woods, seas, clouds, and mountain-ranges: far
> Above the sun, the aethers silver-swanned
> With nebulae, and the remotest star,
> My spirit! with agility you move . . .

> *Au-dessus des étangs, au-dessus des vallées,*
> *Des montagnes, des bois, des nuages, des mers,*
> *Par-delà le soleil, par-delà les éthers,*
> *Par-delà les confins des sphères étoilées,*
> *Mon esprit, tu te meus avec agilité . . .*
>
> ("Elévation," trans. Roy Campbell)

> Come, travel with me in dreams,
> Far, far beyond the range of the possible and the known!

> *Viens! oh! viens voyager dans les rêves,*
> *Au-delà du possible, au-delà du connu!*
>
> ("La Voix," trans. George Dillon)

It is clear that in these two examples (to which one could easily add many others), the mind's motion has as its function neither a participation in cosmic movement nor a self-elevation which might permit it better to embrace the latter. Baudelaire is in no way a poet of the cosmos. He is neither a Dante nor a Milton. He is even less a Lamartine, in whose works poetic movement tends to accompany things in their ascension and flight. In Baudelaire, movement is the mind's flight *far away* from things and simultaneously away from the place where, in the midst of things, the mind risks finding itself forever trapped. In a word, by virtue of his very movement—which is a movement of horror in the face of his present existence—Baudelaire hastens to put as much space as he can between himself and himself. Only through estrangement can he succeed in tolerating himself.

One of Baudelaire's great themes is looking at an object from the greatest possible distance; that is, in spatial or temporal depth, at the edge of the horizon. Speaking of Poe's poems or short stories, Baudelaire notes, "*At the limits of their horizon*, oriental towns and edifices appear, vaporized by the distance, showered by the sun with rains of gold." In an example such as this, the idealization of the landscape depends concomitantly upon a distancing, which makes objects more vaporous, and upon a solar action of disintegration which, drenching the whole of everything in a golden rain, transforms this whole into a multitude of glittering flakes. The sun-star and pure distance collaborate to make objects lose their quality of distinctiveness and to force them into a common background in which they are blurred.

Perhaps the same is true for Baudelairean sunsets as well. Their function is to use distance to engulf not only the light of day but, with it, everything it illuminates: first external objects, and then the mental objects that haunt thought. Thus the sunset is also the setting of human consciousness, its entry into a region of drowsy revery where thought seems gradually to be emptied of its contents:

> Look, the dead years dressed
> in old clothes crowd the balconies of the sky.
> Regret emerges smiling from the sea,
> the sick sun slumbers underneath an arch,
> and like a shroud strung out from east to west,
> listen, my Dearest, hear the sweet night march!

> *Vois se pencher les défuntes Années,*
> *Sur les balcons du ciel, en robes surannées;*
> *Surgir du fond des eaux le Regret souriant;*
> *Le Soleil moribond s'endormir sous une arche,*
> *Et, comme un long linceul traînant à l'Orient,*
> *Entends, ma chère, entends la douce Nuit qui marche.*
>
> ("Recueillement," trans. Robert Lowell)

We seem here to be participating in the very creation of distance, or, what amounts to the same thing, the past. For the most part, the Baudelairean past inhabits the mind in the form of a present past, an eternally living past, which persists in weighing down the mind conscious of it. This present past maintains by its very presence a terrifyingly vivid quality. As we have seen, it is indelible. Such is remorse—intolerable because it preserves in the mind an image that remains all too close and, consequently, a burning presence. And yet, Baudelaire wonders, is it not possible to make this past recede into the background of one's perspective? Then its bitterness will be softened, its cruelty rendered less harsh. In the Baudelairean phenomenon of the sunset we witness this kind of *mise au lointain*, a distancing of things. The past, and with it the long procession of memories that normally accompany it, solemnly withdraw with the sun, so that the sunset, as Baudelaire writes elsewhere, becomes "the marvelous allegory of a soul, laden with life, which sinks behind the horizon with a magnificent stock of thoughts and dreams."

The beauty of the image suggested here lies in the fact that what seems to sink behind the horizon is not only a fragment of life but the totality of an existence. The depth of the perspective is reflected in the length of the procession moving along it. But that is not all. This spiritual plenitude, this totality of being, is, in one sense, a voyage. Like a ship filled with passengers, it trims its sails for a destination so distant that it will soon be impossible to keep it in view. The dominating impression, then, is no longer that of a present past, continuing to make its heaviness and bitterness felt. On the contrary, the past evoked here is anguishing only because it is receding. The Baudelairean memory can then be painful in two ways: at times because it persists in remaining cruelly present; at times, conversely, because it is perceived as being gloomily engulfed by the nonpresent.

Hence the typically plaintive quality of this second experience. Whereas remorse in Baudelaire is always accompanied by bitterness ("the bitter-flowing bile of my ancient grief"), the contemplation of the past from a growing distance inspires a more tranquil sadness, with softer accents. Nevertheless, the sight of "a far world, defunct almost, absent," offers the spectator an image of himself that is profoundly painful since the movement slowly lowering him into death is the image of his own life. And in this contemplation of the self from a distance, across the layers of years, there is for Baudelaire something analogous to a farewell addressed to someone never to be seen again. This is the tone that can be detected in the famous lines:

> How far you are O heaven of delicate scent! . . .
> The simple heaven full of stolen joys,
> Is it so farther than the China seas?

Comme vous êtes loin, paradis parfumé! . . .
L'innocent paradis, plein de plaisirs furtifs,
Est-il déjà plus loin que l'Inde et que la Chine?
("Moesta et errabunda,"
trans. Hilary Corke)

It is indeed with plaintive cries, with a type of modulated sob, that the poet attempts to call back a distant paradise and to animate it with a voice still silver-toned. Nevertheless, the paradise evoked is even farther away than the most distant lands of the Orient. The poet measures the distance separating him from himself, which tends in his eyes to become an absolute distance. Baudelaire is accustomed to those long glances cast over the shoulder. He is the traveler who stops for the night and makes use of the situation to calculate not so much the progress he has made as the span of life already traversed and thus nearly out of reach.

In the poem of the "femmes damnées," Hippolyte's situation is the same:

With tempest-troubled eyes she sought the blue
Heaven of her innocence, how far away!
Like some sad traveller, who turns to view
The dim horizons passed at dawn of day.

Elle cherchait, d'un oeil troublé par la tempête,
De sa naïveté le ciel déjà lointain,
Ainsi qu'un voyageur qui détourne la tête
Vers les horizons bleus dépassés le matin.
("Delphine et Hippolyte,"
trans. Aldous Huxley)

The traveler looking back can be found in numerous passages in Baudelaire's works. In one of the author's earliest poems (probably dated 1840), he speaks of the sweetness of scanning the east for the scarlet hues of a morning long since vanished. Next comes the comment that it is also sweet to "listen to the echoes which sing from behind," that first sonorous image of reverberation which for Baudelaire allow the songs and cries of the past to be heard from afar in the present moment.

There are many more examples. In *Fanfarlo*, another early work, the hero Samuel Cramer describes the disillusionment that separates him from past days: "We are all rather like a traveler who has crossed a very large country and every night looks at the sun, which earlier bathed the charms of the road in gold, setting into a flat horizon." Contemplating the past results in a perception of the platitudinous character of one's present existence, as well as the inaccessibility of one's past. Moreover, every immediate experience, by virtue of its intensity, tends to hollow out an abyss between the present and past. This is the case with Hippolyta, overwhelmed by the shock of the Sapphic experience and unable to perceive of her lost naiveté as anything other than the endlessly withdrawing phantom of a being it no longer is. Such is also the situation of the opium eater, his memory both exalted and vaporized by the stimulant to which he has surrendered his mind: "He is the traveler who turns back, in the evening, toward the land traveled that morning, and who remembers with emotion and sadness the multitude of thoughts that filled his mind while he was crossing those regions now evaporated into horizons.

Thus in Baudelaire the experience of depth can be confused with that of the abyss. Evocation is transformed into evaporation. And, far from offering itself, with each occurrence, as a salvation from anguish and sadness, depth in Baudelaire—and mnemonic depth in particular—frequently reveals itself to be the powerful catalyst of despair. In a quatrain from "Balcon," depth appears as an interior void:

> Can vows and perfume, kisses infinite,
> Be reborn from the gulf we cannot sound;
> As rise to heaven suns once again made bright
> After being plunged in deep seas and profound?

> *Ces serments, ces parfums, ces baisers infinis*
> *Renaîtront-ils d'un gouffre interdit à nos sondes,*
> *Comme montent au ciel les soleils rajeunis*
> *Après s'être lavés au fond des mers profondes?*
> ("Le Balcon," trans. F. P. Sturm)

The answer to this question is sadly negative. In contrast to cosmic phenomena with their inexhaustible power of renewal, psychic phenomena plunge into a chasm in which they cannot find the resources necessary to return full of the vigor they had once possessed. The most important of all experiences in Baudelaire, that of depth, is one not of restoration but of disintegration. It is the disappearance of an existence in that vast, dark region into which all forms of life, thought, emotion, memory, and feeling are soon to sink.

Thus nothing haunts Baudelaire's thoughts more than this immense, eternally gaping interior region. He gives it a name which he even considered giving to his great collection of poetry: "Limbo." Delacroix's painting *Women of Algiers* impressed Baudelaire above all others because he sensed in it affinities with his own mental state. In the painting, he says, he feels "the strong scent of a place of iniquity, which soon guides our thoughts toward the fathomless limbo of sadness." Moreover, the Delacroix painting probably inspired "Delphine et Hippolyte," a poem that presents Sapphic love as the opportunity for its practitioner to discover the abyss of her own thought:

> I feel my inmost being rent, as though
> A gulf had yawned—the gulf that is my heart . . .
> As fire 'tis hot, as space itself profound—

> . . . *Je sens s'élargir dans mon être*
> *Un abîme béant; cet abîme est mon coeur!* . . .
> *Brûlant comme un volcan, profond comme le vide!*
>   ("Delphine et Hippolyte,"
>   trans. Aldous Huxley)

Aided by Delacroix, who opens "immense vistas to the most adventurous imaginations," Baudelaire thus discovers (perhaps not exactly, as Sartre would have it), the nothingness to which all consciousness is brought and more precisely, the "depth of perspective" that is revealed each time consciousness sees aspects of spiritual life—which had at first enriched and animated the same consciousness—disappear into that depth. Depth is not pure vacuity; it is rather an interior spaciosity, the place of all mental activity. This spaciosity is most often revealed in the objects thought chooses to contemplate; but at times it may be within thought itself, in the absence of all objects—like the host who, having given a banquet for numerous guests, finds himself alone in the room they have just vacated. The theme of interior depth then, is linked to that of the survival of the mind after the shapes that had temporarily occupied it. This theme in Baudelaire may have come from the works of Poe, in which it abounds and in which one encounters in every utterance the description of a thought solitarily persisting in the tomb. It is the theme of the living dead, a frequent one in Baudelaire as well:

> But tell me if any torture is left to dread
> For this old soulless body, dead as the dead?

> *Et dites-moi s'il est encor quelque torture*
> *Pour ce vieux corps sans âme et mort parmi les morts?*
>   ("Le Mort joyeux," trans. Jackson Mathews)

The anguish described here does not come from the fact that, after death, the body of the deceased may be destined to endure new tortures.

What is frightening is, rather, that this posthumous torture may include consciousness. Similarly, in calling to mind a figurine by Eugene Christophe, representing a woman hiding her tears behind a mask, Baudelaire asks himself, "But why is she weeping?" He offers himself the following answer:

> She weeps, mad girl, because her life began;
> Because she lives. One thing she does deplore
> So much that she kneels trembling in the dust—
> That she must live tomorrow, evermore,
> Tomorrow and tomorrow—as we must!

> —*Elle pleure, insensé, parce qu'elle a vécu!*
> *Et parce qu'elle vit! Mais ce qu'elle déplore*
> *Surtout, ce qui la fait frémir jusqu'aux genoux,*
> *C'est que demain, hélas! il faudra vivre encore!*
> *Demain, après-demain et toujours!—comme nous!*
> ("Le Masque," trans. Graham Reynolds)

The cause for the sadness expressed here has nothing to do with the objective quality of existence itself. The masked woman is not weeping because of the particular grievances which overwhelm her. She is weeping because the most unbearable of all situations is the one in which life continues indefinitely without in some way being distracted from itself by the events, whatever their nature, that occupy the mind.

In short, at the end of its itinerary, after the series of experiences which it has provided for itself, Baudelaire's thought defines itself in two ways, both similar and opposed: either as pure depth without objects, or as pure activity of mind without reason or end. Who am I, Baudelaire asks. Am I the void I see growing inside me, or am I the movement passing through that void, filling it? Am I to recognize myself in the tragic absence of existence I am leaning over, or in the act by which I conceal this absence from myself?

This is assuredly the furthermost point of thought's movement closing in on itself. Alternatively discovering and fleeing objects, the Baudelairean intellect ultimately finds itself in the presence of a depth that nothing can animate any longer except thought itself: a type of perpetual motion machine running on empty. In this way, to an extent, Baudelairean thought tends to merge with this bare cavity; on the other hand, however, it is capable of seeing itself, vertiginously and in its own mirror, only as a thought which thinks itself, which eternally thinks itself:

The dialogue is dark and clear
When a heart becomes its mirror!

Tête-à-tête sombre et limpide
Qu'un coeur devenu son miroir!
                    ("L'Irrémédiable,"
                    trans. Henry Curwen)

ROSEMARY LLOYD

Baudelaire's Creative Criticism

In one of her more fanciful moments, Enid Starkie pictures what might have been Baudelaire's life had he been an English rather than a French adolescent:

> Baudelaire, at this stage of his life, would have gone up to either Oxford or Cambridge, as an undergraduate where, under proctorial and tutorial supervision, he would have done himself no permanent harm. He would probably have made a name for himself in undergraduate circles, in artistic and literary clubs, and this might have satisfied his need for eccentric self-expression.

Not really, one feels, the way to make a poet. Baudelaire himself, in one of the projected but never completed prefaces to *Les Fleurs du Mal*, suggests that poets can, to some extent at least, be made:

> comment, appuyé sur mes principes et disposant de la science que je me charge de lui enseigner en vingt leçons, tout homme devient capable de composer une tragédie qui ne sera pas plus sifflée qu'une autre, ou d'aligner un poème de la longueur nécessaire pour être aussi ennuyeux que tout poème épique connu.

> [supported by my principles and having at his command the science I have undertaken to teach him in twenty lessons, any

From *French Studies: A Quarterly Review* 36, no. 1 (January 1982). © 1982 by the Society for French Studies. All translations have been made by the editor unless otherwise indicated.

man would become capable of composing a tragedy no worse
than any other, or of coughing up a poem of the length required
to be as boring as any known epic poem.]

Similarly, in a letter to the publisher Lévy in 1862 he mentions his plan to
explain his poetic methods and teach his reader "l'art d'en faire autant [the
art of doing as much]." Yet he adds with sardonic resignation that he may,
after all, lack "le courage d'écrire cette sérieuse bouffonnerie [the courage to
write this serious buffoonery]." However ironic this may be, it certainly
reflects an entrenched nineteenth-century belief in the power of education:
in *L'Education sentimentale* Flaubert's painter Pellerin is discovered reading
all the aesthetic treatises he can lay hands on, in the conviction that knowledge
equals skill, that theory creates technique. The school Baudelaire learnt in
was of course far vaster and far richer: if he himself claimed, in a no doubt
over-quoted and perhaps deliberately provocative assertion, that "De Maistre
et Poe [lui] ont appris à raisonner [De Maistre and Poe had taught him to
think]" his critical reviews reveal how often the writings of others served to
inspire or goad him into aesthetic or psychological questioning, the kind of
questioning that often led to creative writing.

     We are made aware as early as the *Salon de 1846* of the interplay between
art criticism and creativity: there Baudelaire insists that "le meilleur compte
rendu d'un tableau pourra être un sonnet ou une élégie [a sonnet or an elegy
could be the best account given of a painting]." The poems "Le Masque,"
"L'Amour et le crâne" ["Love and the Skull"], and "Une gravure fantastique"
["A Fantastic Engraving"] show him putting this challenging precept into
admirable practice. But what would be the best response to a work not of
plastic art, but of literature, bearing in mind Baudelaire's demand that criticism be "amusante et poétique [amusing and poetic]" and that it reveal the
work of art reflected through "un esprit intelligent et sensible [an intelligent
and sensible mind]"? I would suggest that here Baudelaire uses an analogous
form: among the best passages of his literary criticism—certainly those
which are both amusing and poetic—are penetrating pastiches and revealing
parodies.

     A parody, as the word suggests, sets itself up against literature, against
the *ode*, the song: anti-literature, its first aim is to mock, but in Baudelaire's
case at least it has the underlying aim of correcting certain false premises or
unsound directions in contemporary literature or speech. In his first essay
on Gautier, he inserts a biting parody of what he calls the "détestable et
risible argot [detestable and laughable slang]" common to the *salons* of the
bourgeoisie: "je vous suppose *interné* dans un salon *bourgeois* et prenant le

café, après dîner, avec le *maître* de la maison, la *dame* et ses *demoiselles* [I imagine you *interned* in a *bourgeois* salon and drinking coffee, after dinner, with the *master* of the house, the *lady* and their *young ladies*]." In the study of the *école païenne* [pagan school] the pagan is as cruelly caricatured as those worthy citizens deflated by the sharp point of Daumier's pen:

> Il faut revenir aux vraies doctrines, obscurcies *un instant* par l'infâme Galiléen. D'ailleurs, Junon m'a jeté un regard favorable, un regard qui m'a pénétré jusqu'à l'âme. J'étais triste et mélancolique au milieu de la foule, regardant le cortège et implorant avec des yeux amoureux cette belle divinité, quand un de ses regards, bienveillant et profond, est venu me relever et m'encourager.
> —Junon vous a jeté un de ses regards de vache, *Bôôpis Êrê.*

> [We must return to the true doctrines, only momentarily obscured by that infamous Galilean. Besides, Juno has cast a favorable glance at me, a glance which penetrated to the very depths of my soul. I was sad and melancholy in the midst of the crowd, gazing at the pageant and imploring the beautiful goddess with adoring eyes, when one of her glances, kindly and profound, came to restore and encourage me.
> —Juno cast one of her cowlike gazes on you, Boopis Ere.]

Nevertheless, Baudelaire uses parody only sparingly: it is after all, as he knew all too well after his review of *Prométhée délivré*, a technique that can turn itself into a boomerang. A parody that is too close to the bone is "une flèche qui se retourne, ou au moins vous dépouille la main en partant, une balle dont le ricochet peut vous tuer [an arrow which boomerangs, or, at the very least skins your hand as it flies, a bullet whose ricochet could kill you]."

More subtle than parody, pastiche, that epiphytic flower that grows on the ideas and techniques of another to produce fresh beauty, offers not only a less dangerous weapon but also a useful means of exploration of another's style and refinement of one's own, two purposes for which, of course, Proust exploited it in *Pastiches et Mélanges*. From his earliest reviews, Baudelaire reveals his considerable control of this technique in the delightful "Comment on paie ses dettes quand on a du génie" ["How one pays one's debts when one has genius"], a title which itself recalls a pamphlet due to Balzac's press if not his pen: *L'Art de ne pas payer ses dettes et de satisfaire ses créanciers sans débourser un sou* ["The art of not paying his debts and of satisfying his creditors without giving up a penny"]. In a series of striking pastiches, revealing how well Baudelaire knew his novelist even then, he reflects Balzac's strikingly physical images—"lui, le cerveau poétique tapissé de chiffres comme le cabinet d'un financier [his poetic brain plastered with figures like a financier's office]"—, the deliberate exaggeration of his characters—"l'homme aux faillites mythologiques dont il oublie toujours d'allumer la lanterne [the man of mythic failures, of hyperbolic and fantasmatic enterprises whose lantern he still forgets to light]"—, his belief that a man's outward appearance explains his personality or his mood—"il était triste, à en juger par ses sourcils froncés, sa large bouche moins distendue et moins lippue qu'à l'ordinaire [he was sad, to judge by his knitted brows, his large mouth less distended and less thick-lipped than usual]"—, and his depiction of a society driven by the twin pistons of money and pleasure—"rêvait-il ananas à quatre sous, pont suspendu en fil de liane, villa sans escalier avec des boudoirs tendus en mousseline [did he dream of pineapples for four cents, a suspension bridge of creeper vines, a villa without stairs and boudoirs hung with muslin]?" Titles of Balzac's novels are also punningly incorporated into the text: the writer is described as "le grand pourchasseur de rêves, sans cesse à la *recherche de l'absolu* [the great dream pursuer, unceasingly in search of the absolute]," his brow is so furrowed as to suggest a *"peau de chagrin* [distressed skin]" and the review asks if his grief is caused by "les *Souffrances de l'inventeur* [The Sufferings of the Inventor]." Indeed, the whole article can be seen as an amused, but above all admiring, pastiche of Balzac's *Un grand homme de province à Paris* [*A Great Man of the Provinces in Paris*].

Later, such pastiches are conveyed in a more sober manner. In 1859, for example, Baudelaire echoes Gautier's image-studded style when he recalls his first meeting with the poet: "depuis cette petite fête de ma jeunesse, que d'années au plumage varié ont agité leurs ailes et pris leur vol vers le ciel avide [since that small fête of my youth, what years of varied plummage have beaten their wings and taken flight toward the avid sky]." Yet the sentence closes on an eminently Baudelairean expression: "le ciel avide" recalls "Chant d'automne" ["Autumn Song"] (1859)—"La tombe attend; elle est avide [The grave awaits; she is eager]"—, "Le Cygne" ["The Swan"] (1860) with its reference to "le ciel ironique et cruellement bleu [the ironic and cruelly blue sky]" and "L'Horloge" ["The Clock"] (1860)—*"Souviens-toi* que le Temps est un joueur avide [*Remember* that Time is an avid gambler]." The review of *Madame Bovary*, and above all the passage explaining the nature of Flaubert's novel as a result of contemporary circumstances, allows Baudelaire to evoke several novelists of the time in a series of luminous pastiches, which are all the more challenging for being so concise. The intensity of tone, the antagonism of attitude, the tendency to transform fairly banal characters into heroes of a modern Catholic myth, all these elements of Barbey d'Aurevilly's style are caught like wasps in the amber of a single sentence:

> D'Aurevilly, vrai catholique, évoquant la passion pour la vaincre, chantant, pleurant et criant au milieu de l'orage, planté comme Ajax sur un rocher de desolation et ayant toujours l'air de dire à son rival,—homme, foudre, dieu ou matière—"enlève-moi, ou je t'enlève."

> [D'Aurevilly, a sincere Catholic, evoking passion in order to conquer it, singing, weeping and crying out in the midst of the storm, planted like Ajax on a rock of desolation and forever seeming to say to his rival—man, thunderbolt, god or matter—"destroy me or I will destroy you."]

Champfleury is mentioned in terms which call attention to his tic—already pinpointed by Baudelaire in an earlier review—of repeating a phrase in slightly different terms: he stands accused of having neglected "le lieu commun, le lieu de rencontre de la foule, le rendez-vous public de l'éloquence [the common place, the place of encounter with the crowd, the public meeting-place of eloquence]."

The articles written towards the end of the 1850s for Eugène Crépet's anthology of French poets are also enriched by this process: Hugo's style, as well as the two divisions of *Les Contemplations,* are evoked in the following sentence: "comme Démosthène il converse avec les flots et le vent; autrefois, il rôdait solitaire dans des lieux bouillonnant de vie humaine; aujourd'hui il marche dans des solitudes peuplées par sa pensée" [like Demosthenes he speaks with the waves and the wind; in the past, he prowled alone in places teeming with human life, now he walks in wildernesses peopled by his thought]." The careful balance of the sentence, the vision of the poet as magus, the counterpointing of the antitheses and the somewhat lofty rhetoric are all recognizably Hugolian.

Obviously Baudelaire uses these pastiches in part to aid the more perceptive of his readers, by recalling the style of a well-known writer or suggesting that of someone less familiar. More importantly, however, a pastiche allows him to flex his muscles, not so much as critic, but as creative artist, taking up a theme, an idea, a stylistic device, discovered in the writings of another but that Baudelaire believes he can transform, deepen, enrich. Thus, he seizes an image Balzac often uses to suggest an individual's certainty of future glory, his ability to rise above the crowd—that of the meteor or the aurora borealis. At first the metaphor is applied to Balzac himself: the novelist is "ce prodigieux météore qui couvrira notre pays d'un nuage de gloire, comme un orient bizarre et exceptionnel, comme une aurore polaire inondant le désert glacé de ses lumières féeriques [that prodigious meteor which will cover our land with a cloud of glory, like a bizarre and exceptional east, like a polar dawn inundating the icy desert with its enchanting light]." The image recurs in a poem first published in 1860, entitled "Chanson d'après-midi" ["Afternoon Song"] which concludes with the triumphant quatrain: "Mon âme par toi guérie, / Par toi, lumière et couleur! / Explosion de chaleur / Dans ma noire Sibérie! [My heart healed by you / By you, light and color! / Explosion of heat / In my black Siberia!]." But he transforms the metaphor, making it quintessentially Baudelairean, in the prose poem "Any where out of the world": there, the poet suggests to his soul that they visit the polar regions: "là nous pourrons prendre de longs bains de ténèbres, cependant que, pour nous divertir, les aurores boréales nous enverront de temps en temps leurs gerbes roses, comme des reflets d'un feu d'artifice de l'Enfer [we could take long baths in the shadows there, while, to amuse us, the aurora borealis surrounded us from time to time with its rosy sprays, like the reflections of an artificial fire of Hell]." Balzac would have given us an explicit, generalizing affirmation of the link between beauty and evil: Baudelaire's power lies, at least in part, in the conciseness and allusiveness of his suggestions.

Similar examples of cross-fertilization between creative and critical writing are provided by a metaphor through which Baudelaire suggests the style of Poe. In 1854, he refers to his earlier, mistaken notion that Poe's life had been that of a rich and happy man: "j'ignorais que ces éblouissantes végétations étaient le produit d'une terre volcanisée [I didn't know that these dazzling growths were the product of volcanized earth]." The metaphor reappears in the 1856 introduction to *Histoires extraordinaires*. Referring to the suggestion that Poe might have had affairs with women other than his wife, Baudelaire asks: "y a-t-il lieu de s'étonner qu'un être aussi nerveux, dont la soif du Beau était peut-être le trait principal, ait parfois, avec une ardeur passionnée, cultivé la galanterie, cette fleur volcanique et musquée pour qui le cerveau bouillonnant des poètes est un terrain de prédilection [is it astonishing that so nervous a being, whose thirst for the Beautiful was perhaps his principal trait, cultivated, at times, with impassioned ardor, this volcanic and musky flower for which a poet's seething brain is desired soil]?" A different version of the image occurs in the prose poem "Le Désir de peindre" ["The Desire to Paint"] where the poet evokes a woman in a series of disquieting images, but concludes by asserting: "cependant, au bas de ce visage inquiétant [. . .] éclate avec une grâce inexprimable, le rire d'une grande bouche, rouge et blanche, et délicieuse, qui fait rêver au miracle d'une superbe fleur éclose dans un terrain volcanique [while, at the bottom of this disturbing face . . . the laugh of a large mouth, red and white and delicious, which makes one dream of the miracle of a superb flower blooming in volcanic earth, broke with inexpressible grace]." A second instance is provided by the first full-length presentation of Poe's tales, when Baudelaire suggests that certain men suffer in such a way as to imply that divine beings whip them for the edification of others: "on dirait que l'Ange aveugle de l'expiation s'est emparé de certains hommes et les fouette à tour de bras pour l'édification des autres [it is as if the blind Angel of atonement seized certain men and whips them relentlessly for the edification of others]." Moreover it is this element that Baudelaire stresses in his study of Delacroix's painting of the punishment bestowed on Heliodorus. The image of the angel of vengeance also recurs in two of Baudelaire's poems, "Le Voyage" where even in their sleep the travellers are tormented by curiosity, "Comme un Ange cruel qui fouette des soleils [like a cruel Angel who whips the suns]," and "Le Rebelle" ["The Rebel"] with its arresting opening lines:

> Un Ange furieux fond du ciel comme un aigle,
> Du mécréant saisit à plein poing les cheveux,
> Et dit, le secouant: "Tu connaîtras la règle!"

> [An angry Angel plunges out of the sky
> Grips the sinner's hair and shakes him hard,
> Shouting: "Hear and obey, it is the law!"
> (Richard Howard. *The Flowers of Evil*. Boston:
> David R. Godine, Publisher, Inc., 1982)]

Poe is important in another context, apart from that of images reappearing in both the creative and the critical writing: in one of his theoretical studies, he insists on the need to begin whatever one is writing in a striking manner: "How many good books suffer neglect through the inefficiency of their beginnings! It is far better that we commence irregularly, immethodically, than that we fail to arrest the attention [. . .]. At all risks, let there be a few vivid sentences *imprimis*, by way of the electric bell to the telegraph." Baudelaire seems to take this up in his *Journaux intimes*, in one of those frequent, deeply moving, injunctions to himself to get down to work: "début d'un roman, commencer un sujet n'importe où et, pour avoir envie de le finir, débuter par de très belles phrases [beginning of a novel, to begin the subject no matter where and, in order to arouse the desire to finish it, to

begin with very beautiful phrases]." A comparison of the opening sentences
of the three main studies on Poe reveals Baudelaire carrying this out, per-
fecting the art of the *entrée en matière*. The first study begins: "Il y a des
destinées fatales; il existe dans la littérature de chaque pays des hommes qui
portent le mot *guignon* écrit en caractères mystérieux dans les plis sinueux
de leurs fronts [There are fatal destinies; in the literature of each country
there are men who wear the words *bad luck* written in mysterious characters
in the sinuous folds of their foreheads]." This becomes more striking in the
1856 preface: "dans ces derniers temps, un malheureux fut amené devant
nos tribunaux, dont le front était illustré d'un rare et singulier tatouage: *Pas
de chance!* [recently, an unfortunate man was sent to court, on his forehead
a rare and strange tatoo was drawn: No luck!]"; while the third notice, by
far the most aggressive of them, opens explosively: "*Littérature de décadence!*—
Paroles vides que nous entendons souvent tomber, avec la sonorité d'un
bâillement emphatique, de la bouche de ces sphinx sans énigme qui veillent
devant les portes saintes de l'Esthétique classique [Literature of decadence!—
Empty words which we often hear fall, with the sonority of a pompous
yawn, from the mouths of those unenigmatic sphinxes who keep watch before
the sacred doors of classical Aesthetics]."

   To some extent, too, those resounding opening lines that mark so much
of the creative and critical writing reflect a belief that seems to become more
and more firmly fixed in Baudelaire's mind as the articles develop: the awareness of great art as a *gageure* [wagering], as a wager the writer undertakes in
choosing a theme or technique of singular recalcitrance. It is in terms of the
gageure that Baudelaire presents Flaubert selecting the theme and setting of
Madame Bovary or Gautier deciding to retell the familiar story of Gyges's
ring precisely because of its familiarity. This offers an accurate reflection of
Baudelaire's own approach, firstly to creative writing, but secondly of course
to criticism. Certainly the prefatory letter to *Le Spleen de Paris* suggests the
element of *gageure* he saw in that undertaking: "quel est celui de nous qui
n'a pas, dans des jours d'ambition, rêvé le miracle d'une prose poétique
[which one of us, in his moments of ambition, has not dreamed of the miracle
of poetic prose (*Paris Spleen*. Louise Varèse, trans. New York: New Directions Publishing Co., 1970)]."

   Indeed, the subtle yet firm relationship between Baudelaire's articles
and his poetry is perhaps most evident and most stimulating in connexion
with his experiments in prose poetry. Although his reasons for turning to
this relatively unfamiliar genre were complex and stem from the doubts and
despair of the late 1850s, he transformed verse poetry into prose poetry as
early as 1851, when the poems on wine "L'Ame du vin" ["The Soul of

Wine"] and "Le Vin des chiffonniers" ["Ragpicker's Wine"] reappear in prose form in the study of wine and hashish. Clearly prose poetry was not a form of *pis aller*, a confession of defeat, but a creative medium more suited to certain themes and purposes. These purposes could be closely associated with literary criticism as Baudelaire saw it—not that of an Olympian judge assessing merit from on high, but that of a participant in the struggle, only too willing to leap into the ring himself to show how a certain blow might be struck, how a certain mood or effect might be created. If, in his literary criticism, he debates the theoretical questions behind the creation of the prose poems and experiments with images, situations or themes that appear, transposed, in *Le Spleen de Paris*, the notice he wrote on Marceline Desbordes-Valmore is a prose poem in its own right, concentrating less, particularly in the final paragraph, on conventional analysis than on distilling the essence and evoking the atmosphere of her poetry.

It begins, like many of the prose poems, by posing in immediate, personal terms, a question of general interest: how can one explain an enthusiasm which apparently contradicts both one's normal reactions and one's cherished theories? He asks:

> Plus d'une fois un de vos amis, comme vous lui faisiez confidence d'un de vos goûts ou d'une de vos passions, ne vous a-t-il pas dit: "Voilà qui est singulier! car cela est en complet désaccord avec toutes vos autres passions et avec votre doctrine?"

> [More than once hasn't one of your friends, as you were confiding in him one of your inclinations or one of your passions, said: "That's odd! It's completely out of step with your doctrine and all of your other passions?"]

One thinks of the opening lines of the prose poem "Perte d'auréole" ["The Lost Halo"]: "Eh quoi! vous ici mon cher? Vous, dans un mauvais lieu! [. . .] En vérité, il y a là de quoi me surprendre [What? You're here, my friend? You, in such a rundown place! This is really a surprise]!" Yet one also thinks, such is Baudelaire's power to suggest works written by those he reviews, of Desbordes-Valmore's own poem "La Prière perdue":

> Inexplicable coeur, énigme de toi-même,
> Tyran de ma raison, de la vertu que j'aime.

> [Inexplicable heart, closed to yourself,
> Tyrant of my reason, of the virtue that I love.
>   "The Lost Prayer"]

The article's concluding paragraph is the kind of *tour de force* in which Baudelaire obviously revels, opening on a quietly confiding note, building up through the elaborate comparison and closing with a resounding affirmation of the permanent youthfulness of Desbordes-Valmore's poetry. The metaphor, in which the atmosphere of the poetry is evoked through comparison with external nature, could, moreover, serve to illustrate the theoretical discussion of "la *correspondance* et [le] symbolisme universels" that recurs in the studies of Poe, Hugo and Gautier.

Similarly, the passage in the review of Hugo where Baudelaire, himself a meteor exploring the vast poetic possibilities of space, raises a series of rich, provocative questions about the universe, can be seen as a prose poem embedded in the matrix of more traditional literary criticism. Certainly the brief study of Le Vavasseur—two paragraphs weaving variations around the basic theme of the poet as both physical gymnast and ringmaster of rhyme and rhythm—is very similar in tone and technique to several of the prose poems in which the poet appears as jester or gymnast.

Baudelaire's critical reviews are both assessments of, and responses to, the works of other writers: but even more importantly they provide an arena in which he flexes his muscles, trains his reactions, sharpens his awareness of language and stimulates that queen of faculties, his imagination.

BERNARD HOWELLS

Baudelaire: Portrait of the Artist in 1846

There are perhaps half a dozen references in [Baudelaire's novel] *La Fanfarlo* to acting, to posing in front of a mirror, to aping feelings, and many more scattered throughout Baudelaire's work: "Avec ce diable d'homme, le grand problème est toujours de savoir où le comédien commence [With this devil of a man, the biggest problem is always knowing where the actor begins]." One of the many ironies of the end of the story lies in the way [its main character] Cramer is caught out by his own pretence: "Il avait souvent singé la passion; il fut contraint de la connaître [He had often aped passion; he was forced to feel it]." And the passage from imaginary to real is heavy with inescapable material consequences. Reviewing events, the protagonist concludes with a non-conclusion: "Nos passions sont-elles bien sincères? qui peut savoir sûrement ce qu'il veut et connaître au juste le baromètre de son coeur [Aren't our emotions completely sincere? Who could know with certainty what he wants and read accurately the barometer of his heart]?" The strongest passions, then, and the most naïve forms of "credulity" (like the most inextricable forms of commitment) appear to be born in the imagination out of very uncertain origins. In the context which raises the whole question of *la faculté comédienne* [The Acting Faculty] we are told of Cramer that "Comme il avait été dévot avec fureur, il était athée avec passion [As he had been furiously devout, so he was passionately atheist]." The potential "pape militaire [military leader]," the "âme sainte [saintly soul]," the reactionary

From *French Studies: A Quarterly Review* 37, no. 4 (October 1983). © 1983 by the Society for French Studies. All translations have been made by the editor unless otherwise indicated.

disciple of Joseph de Maistre is one role played intermittently by the "parfait comédien [perfect actor]." To grasp fully Baudelaire's attitudes to religion we need to understand in what circumstances and at what points, not just chronologically but in the strata of his psychology, violent emotional and moral conviction is generated in imagination out of a fundamental self-directed irony, that is out of radical self-doubt. There is a great deal in *La Fanfarlo* to support Sartre's contention that the real division in Baudelaire's experience was not between good and evil but between consciousness and nature (including his own nature). A deep-seated irony is part of Cramer's *naïveté* yet threatens to subvert that *naïveté* by calling into doubt the very notion of a natural identity.

Mme de Cosmelly's own histrionic talents are considerable but they are not radical; they are resolutely in the service of a bourgeois ideal of natural virtue viewed by Cramer with a characteristic mixture of reverence and cynicism. Both are "credulous" in different ways. In both cases credulity is the sign of a certain imaginativeness and the source of real misfortune. At the same time the reference to "deux êtres dont les destinées complices ont élevé l'âme à un égal diapason [two beings in which entwined destinies had raised the soul to an equal pitch]" is ironical, given the tissue of misunderstandings between them, and is intended to underline the romantic banality of the situation. Later in the *novella* La Fanfarlo appears as the real (i.e. sensual) feminine counterpart of the hero in a deliberate inversion of the Platonic myth. Mme de Cosmelly shares with Cramer a past nostalgically evoked: "le beau temps [. . .] où notre âme ne raisonnait pas, mais où elle vivait et jouissait [the good times . . . when our soul didn't reason, but when she lived and enjoyed]." But he has changed and she confesses she no longer understands him. She is perplexed by the moral and aesthetic paradoxes of *Les Orfraies* [*The Ospreys*], which seem to repudiate deliberately everything healthy, "normal" and happy. By way of response Cramer undertakes a familiar defence of the poet. He is not an isolated case, he says, but is typical of writers of his generation. The poet chooses to live in an imaginary world as an escape from moral lucidity about himself and about others. The very cult of artificiality is a protest against the corruption of nature. Ordinary men have an unquestioning acceptance of life which is reflected in, and indeed made possible by, the clichés they use. The poet perturbs language in an attempt to get to grips with human reality. But knowledge means we can no longer believe in our own instinctive feelings. Our lucidity is so great it ends up making us humanly stunted; we have no aptitude for life left. The results of disillusionment are spiritual debauchery and emotional impotence. The blame for this state of affairs is laid on the process of culture. We are part of a civilization that is growing old and impotent. We were born crippled; the next generation and its works will be still-born. Allusions to Romantic literature, to Chateaubriand, Musset and Sainte-Beuve for example, proliferate in this section of the text and some pages later all this is referred to as "jargon romantique." The revolt against cliché, Baudelaire is suggesting, has produced its own clichés. Romanticism is already producing its own *chic* and *poncif* to use the terminology of the *Salon*. How is originality to extricate itself from this and survive in a culture crippled by its own self-awareness? Baudelaire's irony does not preclude seriousness; it is an intensification of the nihilism whose postures it mocks. It seeks to relativise Romantic nihilism from the other side of a very thin dividing-line; by accentuating the paradoxical and tragi-comic aspects of a situation that is envisaged only as worsening. In his irony we can detect the persistence of instinctive belief in certain moral values (lucidity, sincerity, authenticity, for example) within an intellectual scepticism that cannot account for belief.

Modern culture, Baudelaire implies in the *Salon de 1846*, is a culture in mourning. Modern man's dress, he suggests, is, symptomatically, undertaker's black: "le frac funèbre et convulsionné que nous endossons tous [in the funereal and tortured frock-coat which we all wear today]," and that is because "nous célébrons tous quelque enterrement [we are each of us celebrating some funeral (Charles Baudelaire, *Art in Paris 1845–1862*. Jonathon Mayne, trans. London: Phaidon Press Ltd., 1965. Hereafter referred to as Mayne)]." The practised eye can discern this spiritual grief and its implications in all the manifestations of modern life. It provides the modern artist with material every bit as "epic" or "heroic" as antiquity, though in a more subtle, sober and complex fashion. It is the source of the emotional colouring specific to the nineteenth-century ideal of Beauty. What we are mourning is, of course, the death of ideals, of permanent truth, or moral stability; the loss in all spheres of the possibility of positive belief, which can in turn be traced back to the death of the sustaining religious myth of our culture. This sense of religious loss accounts for Romantic melancholy, "cette haute et sérieuse mélancolie [this lofty and serious melancholy]," "la douleur morale [moral pain]"; an endemic spiritual sado-masochism which is best expressed in the paintings of Delacroix. Moreover Baudelaire suggests obliquely that if Delacroix, a free-thinker, produced virtually the only contemporary religious painting worth speaking of, one of the reasons for this is the profound affinity between the Romantic sense of tragic loss and the great set-pieces where Christianity celebrates the death of its God; the *Pietà* or *Christ in the Garden of Olives* for example. Delacroix managed to achieve self-expression within the particularities of a difficult cultural moment; other artists, indeed the majority, Baudelaire believes, are foundering. This is not to propose any simple connection between the crisis of atheism in the nineteenth century and the absence of a common belief or the erosion of belief in self to which Baudelaire attributes everything that is wrong in nineteenth-century art. But it *is* to suggest that Baudelaire, like many of his contemporaries, saw the religious crisis as one of the root causes. Can we speak of a crisis of atheism in Baudelaire's own life in 1846? There is evidence both for and against. The article on Ménard for example is curiously ambiguous: the reference to "le culte de la Nature, cette grande religion de Diderot et d'Holbach, cet unique ornement de l'athéisme [the cult of Nature, that great religion of Diderot and Holbach, that only ornament of atheism]" suggests in effect a position closer to atheism than to belief, but an atheism viewed as the disappointing legacy of the Enlightenment. And there is the reference in *La Fanfarlo*: "Comme il avait été dévot avec fureur, il était athée avec passion [As he had been furiously devout, so he was passionately atheist]." But whether Baudelaire was, in 1846, "athée avec passion [passionately atheist]" or not, one can certainly speak of a crisis, and an enduring one, if only in the sense of a dramatic awareness of alternatives which undermines any sense of stability or permanence of conviction. David Kelley, in his study of the context of Baudelaire's *Salon*, shows how aware contemporary art critics were of the ways in which questions of aesthetic allegiance implied larger questions of political and ideological commitment. The Constitutional Monarchy was an attempt to solve disunity by a form of political eclecticism ("la politique du juste milieu [the politics of the happy medium]") and it fostered eclecticism in every other sphere: in philosophy, religion and art. In the political sphere, for example, one might argue that disintegrating eclecticism brought self-doubt to the surface and paradoxically produced extremism. Baudelaire's apparent *volte-face* [about-face] in 1848 followed by his complete detachment from politics after 1852 were themselves symptomatic of the instability of the *régime* that foundered and we should add these reasons to the others (literary and temperamental) alleged in *Mon Coeur mis à nu* ["My Heart Laid Bare"] for Baudelaire's "ivresse en 1848 [drunkenness in 1848]."

The bravado implied by Baudelaire's prescription "la critique doit être partiale, passionnée, politique c'est-à-dire faite à un point de vue exclusif [criticism must be partial, impassioned, political, that is to say, made from an exclusive point of view]" and by his championing of Delacroix is both the product of, and a form of self-defence against, the uncertainties of a culture he thought to be in dissolution. "Le doute est aujourd'hui dans le monde moral la cause principale de toutes les affections morbides [Doubt is the principal cause of all morbid affections in the moral world today]."

Baudelaire's critical admirations and hatreds in the *Salon* betray a fundamental anguish not just about the fortunes of art but about the definition of the individual and of nineteenth-century man. Scheffer is selected as prime target because he summarizes in his mediocrity all the symptoms of a highly contagious cultural disease. Great painters like Delacroix, Baudelaire suggests, believe passionately and exclusively in their own kind of self-expression and therefore in their own style. But painters who are unsure of what they feel become eclectics and "un éclectique n'est pas un homme [an eclectic is no man (Mayne)]." Eclecticism indicates an absence of human reality. It betrays an uncertainty about identity which is the root cause of impotence and which in its modern form is encouraged by the excessive degree of intellectual reflection implicit in Romantic relativism, in its historical and aesthetic aspects. "Des gens qui se donnent si largement le temps de la réflexion ne sont pas des hommes complets; il leur manque une passion [People who are so lavish with their time for reflection are not complete men: they lack the element of passion (Mayne)]." Moreover "le doute revêt une foule de formes; c'est un Protée qui souvent s'ignore lui-même [doubt assumes a whole host of forms; it is a Proteus which often does not recognize its own face (Mayne)]"—in the aesthetic and the moral spheres which are intimately connected. Eclecticism can refer to the general proliferation of imitative schools in the nineteenth century (neo-pagan, neo-Christian, etc.). It may involve borrowing stylistic tricks from a variety of sources: "se faire un caractère par un système d'emprunts contradictoires [(seeking) to make a personality for themselves by a system of contradictory borrowings (Mayne)]." It also designates a deliberate mingling of techniques, colour and line for example, which Baudelaire thinks tend, at their extremes, to exclude each other since they correspond to different temperamental attitudes to the world. Finally eclecticism refers to the confusion of methods appropriate to the different arts, such as painting and literature. Scheffer's "sentimentality" is part of his "literariness" and involves, therefore, a double inauthenticity: that of trying to create an impact by means not specific to painting itself and that of "aping" emotional responses one has outgrown. It is necessarily unfaithful to the conditions of the modern sensibility. Scheffer escapes from the problem of expressing the modern sensibility in one way. Vernet escapes into anecdote, cliché and an official chauvinism whose appeal will not outlive the colonial campaigns and which is a travesty of what Baudelaire means by that difficult and fertile ideal, "une passion exclusive."

Baudelaire, of course, in the *Salon*, is primarily concerned with the implications of personal and collective self-doubt in the aesthetic sphere. In "Des Ecoles et des Ouvriers" ["On Schools and Journeymen" (Mayne)] he

sums up his views on the apparent failure of Romanticism: "le doute, ou
l'absence de foi et de naïveté est un vice particulier à ce siècle [. . .] la
naïveté, qui est la domination du tempérament dans la manière, est un
privilège divin dont presque tous sont privés [Doubt, or the absence of faith
and of *naïveté*, is a vice particular to this age . . . *naïveté*, which means the
dominion of temperament within manner, is a divine privilege which almost
all are without (Mayne)]." The difference between the Classical period and
the Romantic is one of unity. The concrete expression of the common ideological and aesthetic faith that made Classicism a unity was the formation
of great schools around Raphael, around Poussin, and the creation of a
"Grand Manner" which dominated European art for some three hundred
years. Classicism had a unity which only in its decadent academic phase
degenerated into uniformity. On the other hand, Romanticism so far has
produced, not schools in the proper sense, but a diversity of sectarian op-
position-groups which, Baudelaire complained in *Qu'est-ce que le romantisme?*
["What is Romanticism?" (ed.)], had deadened the impact of the Romantic
revolution in France by splitting it up and fighting the battle against Neo-
classicism on a number of separate narrow fronts, each distorted by theoretical over-specialization. The names of these fronts were Realism, Art for
Art's sake, "Catholic" Romanticism, medievalism, local colour, etc. The
retreat into specialisms offered an easy way of avoiding the problem of real
Romantic art, which is "dans la manière de sentir," and is symptomatic of
an individual and general failure to achieve a synthesis. In the classical period
there had been "des écoles [schools]," in the nineteenth century there were
merely "des ouvriers émanicipés [emancipated journeymen]"; and a school
is "une foi, c'est-à-dire l'impossibilité du doute [a faith—that is, the impossibility of doubt (Mayne)]"—the very opposite of eclecticism. Baudelaire's
thinking in the penultimate chapter of the *Salon* is paradoxical but extraor-
dinarily coherent. The essence of it is already contained in his initial formula:
"l'individualisme bien entendu [general individualism (ed.)]." Some further
implications of the "bien entendu" are now spelt out. He believes that *naïveté*
or proper self-expression is possible only within broadly established flexible
conventions of meaning appropriate to a given age. Self-expression is not
possible without reference to some kind of common framework or language.
As Malraux pointed out, in attempting to analyse a cultural crisis very similar
to that facing Baudelaire, the quality of individualism is paradoxically dependent on the quality of the society that nourishes it. The converse of the
paradox is that cultural anarchy leads to loss of strong individualism; in other
words it leads straight to eclecticism and self-doubt. Microcosm mirrors
macrocosm; Baudelaire saw that, like his own personality, Romanticism was

an extremely unstable cultural form. Its *naïveté*, too, was a delicate balance that had to be maintained within the tensions of its own paradoxes. Romanticism in his view stood for the kind of relativism which needed to have absolute confidence in its own worth; this was what made it so exhilarating and so fragile. Baudelaire in 1846 felt that the balance had tipped from exhilaration to fragility; that Romanticism had produced a cultural anarchy where only the very strongest, like Delacroix, could and therefore *should* survive, as well perhaps as a few exotic plants that had managed to adapt precariously: "Quelques excentriques, sublimes et souffrants, compensent mal ce désordre fourmillant de médiocrités [A few sublime and long-suffering eccentrics are poor compensation for this swarming chaos of mediocrity (Mayne)]." *La Fanfarlo* would suggest that Baudelaire classifies himself amongst this eccentric minority. There is a whiff of cultural fascism about *Des Ecoles et des Ouvriers* which will not surprise the reader attentive to the undercurrents of Baudelaire's sensibility in 1846: eclecticism must be put down; the purpose of life is to produce culture, a coherent, unified culture in which self is sustained and nourished and irresolution pacified. Out of this need for form and coherence grew a number of convictions—for example, later on, the belief in dandyism as a kind of alternative society, an exclusive club with strict rules for uncompromising individualists. But the form this need for coherence took in 1846, one of its most enduring forms, was the hero-worship of Delacroix, which itself takes on something of the status of a (vicarious) "passion exclusive."

In the economy of the *Salon*, it is not just the chapters on Romanticism and colour but, perhaps even more so, the "negative" chapters which "conduisent droit à EUGÈNE DELACROIX [lead straight to Eugène Delacroix]." Since *Le peintre de la vie moderne* ["Painting from Modern Life"] there is among critics an almost automatic tendency to equate Baudelaire's preoccupation with modernity with his praise of Guys. But it is Delacroix who appeared first of all to Baudelaire as a symbol of success within modernity, of a more difficult and perhaps, from the writer's point of view, a more enviable kind. Delacroix's modernity is one of feeling not of subject matter; in the latter sense Baudelaire in 1846 is still looking for "le peintre de la vie moderne." But whether academic critics recognize him or not and whether he himself is aware of it or not, Delacroix's quality of feeling makes him "le vrai peintre du XIXe siècle [the true painter of the nineteenth century]." "J'ignore s'il est fier de sa qualité de romantique; mais sa place est ici, parce que la majorité du public l'a depuis longtemps, et même dès sa première oeuvre, constitué le chef de l'école *moderne* [I do not know if he is proud of his title of "romantic," but his place is here, because a long time ago—from his very first work, in fact—the majority of the public placed him at the head of the *modern* school (Mayne)]." Baudelaire returns time and again to the fertile coincidence of Delacroix with his historical moment: "Ôtez Delacroix, la grande chaîne de l'histoire est rompue et s'écoule à terre [Take away Delacroix, and the great chain of history is broken and slips to the ground (Mayne)]." The indissolubility of self and history is implicit in *naïveté*, but like all values, authenticity for Baudelaire has to be striven for. It is the quality of authenticity that Baudelaire admired most in Delacroix, and *La Fanfarlo* would suggest that his admiration depended as much on a perception of differences as of similarities.

Baudelaire admired and even envied Delacroix, because he imagined him to possess the confident, single-minded belief in his own feelings which enabled him to produce abundantly. It is unlikely that in 1846 Baudelaire knew much about Delacroix's own creative difficulties, which were anyway of a different kind; less a matter of inhibition than of coordinating emotional violence. For Baudelaire in the *Salon*, Delacroix is a complete painter because he is a complete man. He has the kind of dominant temperament that transforms experience in a consistent, unified fashion and gives his paintings that strong subjective coherence which Baudelaire seeks as an alternative to the contingency of nature and, indeed, as *Des Ecoles et des Ouvriers* suggests, to the disarray of contemporary culture. And he works unhampered by the kind of critical self-definition which, Baudelaire sensed, could lead to preconceptions that inhibit *naïveté*. The cohabitation of writer and critic in Baudelaire was not without internal tensions.

Other reasons for Baudelaire's cult of Delacroix relate of course to the different nature of the arts practised. A comparison of *La Fanfarlo* and the *Salon* inevitably raises the question of the writer's fascination with the non-conceptual arts ("Glorifier le culte des images (ma grande, mon unique, ma primitive passion) [To glorify the cult of images (my greatest, my only, my primative passion)]") and the privileged status within the Romantic revolution he seems to accord to painting in 1846. But that is another, closely related, story. What I have tried to outline here, starting from *La Fanfarlo*, is the vital emotional argument behind the *Salon* and indeed behind Baudelaire's production as a whole. The early prose texts have an intellectual finesse and buoyancy which hardened later on, with an increasingly tragic sense of failure to achieve a unified self-understanding, into the tendency to seek emotional reassurance in polarities. The "immortelle antithèse philosophique, la contradiction essentiellement humaine [immortal philosophic antithesis, the essentially human contradiction (Mayne)]," the dual "règnes tumultueux d'Ormuz et d'Ahrimane [tumultuous reigns of Ormuzd and Ahriman

(Mayne)]" are later reinstated in all their intractableness. We must not make the mistake of interpreting the early Baudelaire in terms of the later, but neither must we artificially separate them. The tragic dualisms of the *Journaux intimes* are potentially present in the Baudelaire of 1846 as part of "L'empire familier des ténèbres futures [familiar empire of future glooms]," that is as the threat underlying hubristic irony and the search for unity. All the polarities of the later texts are subsumed within that fundamental polarity, which has a somewhat different status, perceived with uncanny accuracy in the opening entry of *Mon Coeur mis à nu:* "De la vaporisation et de la centralisation du *Moi.* Tout est là ["My Heart Laid Bare": Of the vaporization and centralization of *Moi.* Everything is there]."

MARY ANN CAWS

Insertion in an Oval Frame:
Poe Circumscribed by Baudelaire

> . . . *it has always appeared to me that a close circumscription of space is*
> *absolutely necessary to the effect of insulated incident—it has the force of a*
> *frame to a picture.*
>   —EDGAR ALLAN POE, "The Philosophy of Composition"

1. INSERTING AND CIRCUMSCRIBING

In the garden variety of narrative frames, a work is simply inserted within another of the same genre and sort: in a Shakespeare play, we see a play; in a James tale, we read a tale; in a Watteau painting, we observe a painting. Narrators and narratees, explicit and implied, present or putative, abound, but the kind of reading competence necessary is of one kind only.

More challenging for the practitioners of narrative voices within voices and texts within texts is the literary hybrid: within a play, a tale is recounted; within a novel, a play or film is described or said to be acted out or shot; within a poem or a tale, a painting, invented or real, is "shown." The picture I want to get in focus here is a double hybrid, being the translation of a tale by a celebrated poet, the leftovers of whose translation can be seen, in one light and with a properly obsessed observation, to make a poem whose very topos is that of the painting recounted and inserted in the primary tale. The painting thus becomes the visual developing object verbally recounted in all these three texts until it is triply translated: from the original language to the second one, from the second language to a third text, and from its visual impact to a verbal one. The complex tale tells both loss and gain, as a gradual

From *The French Review* 56, no. 5 (April 1983) and from *The French Review* 56, no. 6 (May 1983). © 1983 by the American Association of Teachers of French. "A Phantom" from *Flowers of Evil*, translated by Richard Howard. © 1982 by Richard Howard.

owning and disowning are worked out, through the roles of the painting and narrating subjects and their painted object, whose own subject loses, one after the other, her tongue, her reality, and her life, in order to gain the "life-likeliness" bestowed upon her in translation, by the very act of possession and dispossession.

Around a picture included in a text, the metaphor of circumscription can work itself out fittingly. To write about or around a text—to circumscribe it—is to frame its likeness. It is at once set in relation to the other pictures in the place in which it is found and "insulated," as Poe would have it, and Ortega after him, comparing as he does in *Meditaciones del marco* the frame to an isolating border. Texts translated or shifted sideways may be considered, to that extent, resketched or reframed, reset in a new isolation that may be the life or the death of the picture.

As a double illustration of that pictorial metaphor, I shall take not just an ordinary painting inside a tale, but a portrait inside a text it entitles and gives life to, together with the poetic translation of that picture-in-a-text and the text-around-a-picture to show in what sense its non-literality is both murderous and creative. The slippage within the translation—what it does not manage to or want to possess in the text—is itself the creator of another text whose portrait is verbally and ardently framed.

The following meditation focuses on the substance of Baudelaire's sighting of Poe in its losses and profits, returns to its pointers and its obsessions, and takes its own form from the oblique look, the oval shape, and the circular or framing scription—the circumscription—of the included portrait, unforgettable as the foregrounded object. It is, at once, a meditation on a way of reading certain texts, both obsessed and oblique, circular and passionate, destruction of linearity and logic, but perhaps, as it is responsive to both the death and life-giving forces of the translating impulse, pictorially creative.

2. TELLING AND RETELLING

Poe's tale "The Oval Portrait" forces a deliberately circumscribed focus on the reading of its inserted and principal object. The reader's gaze is trained in the same way as that of the narrator, within a range progressively narrower, moving in from dark corridors to dark room to dark-curtained bed, the latter providing an imaginatively suggestive, if gloomy, position from which to contemplate the portrait of the young bride upon the wall. In that bed is found, providentially placed upon the pillow, the explanatory tale for the portrait. Placed there "by chance," this written counterpart to the visual object determines a simultaneous parallel reading between the portrait, which catches the light, and its own verbal enlightenment, the text in the volume.

What the picture pictures is in fact loss, while it seems to have life, and because of that; the painter of the elaborately framed portrait is the lady's husband, so loving and so much an artist that his admiring brush has stripped the real bride of her life's blood to place the color on the canvas, life upon the wall, and death within his bed. The inserted tale ends there, with no return to the outside frame for the narrator, as if the recounted drama of the exchange of life for truth in representation were in fact to operate in much same way within the text of the tale itself.

Baudelaire takes entire possession of this text and this bride, so that his reading is equivalent to a reframing. The encounter between Poe's story and its French rendering suggests some instructive relations between reading, retelling, translating, and framing.

In a Gothic castle—"one of those piles of commingled gloom and grandeur" fancied by Mrs. Radcliffe—deep within the enclosure and some remote turret, in a small apartment whose walls are hung with many "very spirited modern paintings in frames of rich golden arabesque," a wounded man seeks refuge, in a delirious fever. Bidding his servant close the shutters and throw open the heavy black velvet curtains around his bed, he contemplates the pictures, looks at a small volume left providentially upon his pillow, which tells their stories, and moves the candelabrum, whose position displeases him. The beam of light falls on the portrait of a maiden, so full of "life-likeliness" that had it not been for the peculiar style of vignetting, as of a Sully portrait, and the frame, "oval, richly gilded and filigreed in Moresque," he would have mistaken it *for the maiden herself*. He replaces the candelabrum, thus casting the portrait back into the shadow, and takes up the volume to read the story of that painting, couched in "vague and quaint words" within the written text. The narration has then two levels of discourse and two styles: the "ordinary" or extraordinary style of Poe, and this inserted "other style," for tale and portrait, thus *set*. From this told story and its heavy frame, there is no exit, nor from the bed, nor from the castle.

Of this intensely claustrophobic atmosphere Baudelaire renders a French version, but the original tale is, like the portrait, so "very spirited" that what is left over from the supposed correspondence of translation remains in supplement, its spirit returning two years later in the framing of another text. The translation is in fact already a framing of the doubly-framed initial text, so deeply inset in its heavily-marked contours: within the typical Radcliffean Gothic universe, within the thick castle walls, within the room so remote, within the heavy-curtained bed, within the ornate frame, within the volume, within the tale as told within the volume.

Baudelaire's representation of the Poe tale and portrait sets it still further in, or at a further remove. The peculiarity not just of Poe's design, but of

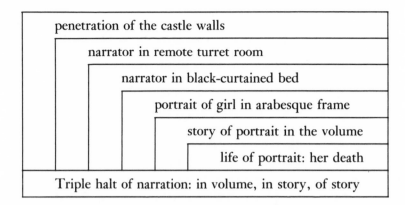

penetration of the castle walls

narrator in remote turret room

narrator in black-curtained bed

portrait of girl in arabesque frame

story of portrait in the volume

life of portrait: her death

Triple halt of narration: in volume, in story, of story

Baudelaire's redesigning of the textual picture, has, quite like the inserted vignette, a force of circumscription and constriction sufficient to set it apart from "real life," but also from "ordinary art." The story so written around or circumscribed, so framed, has all the strength of the "insulated incident" Poe wanted in his close "circumscription of space": the vignette is preserved living even as life is lost.

Baudelaire's own art of translation can be seen, strangely, to take the colors from the cheeks of Poe's own portrait and enframing text, to reframe the story and the model, and, eventually, to make yet another lifelike canvas, in a future poem.

But what of the portrait? Baudelaire's poem *Un Fantôme* seems to include what his translation of Poe's tale excluded, as if, in fact, his rendering or reframing were to have drained off the lifeblood of the tale for his own purpose. Translation is in no sense here any effort at mimesis, but rather a circumspection of the text that then results in circumscribing it, reframing it as object come to death, or then to life. As Poe has translated the oval portrait into words, as his enframed painter has translated the live girl into death and the dead painting into life, giving life to his text by recounting the life-draining of another act, so Baudelaire in his turn drains Poe's text for his own obsessive engulfing of both objects: visual and lifelike, verbal and deathlike, embedding and enframing them in his parallel translation as it steals and recovers. Then, as a guilt working itself out, he recounts his own story of frame and dying-into-life and only later translates the story of the erotic *process of embedding* itself: "So much depends on lying close." In this process of translation, a poetic text is engendered.

3. EMBEDDING OF THE PORTRAIT

The relation between translation and framing finds a peculiar example in this encounter. After all, the violent obsession with reading the visual and verbal portraits, on the part of the narrator so feverishly embedded and curtained in, entails the entire question not just of language but of gaze; in opening and shutting his eyes upon the oval portrait that is the focus of the tale, the speaker who is also the reader gains time for thought and manages to fix his contemplation upon exterior appearance, as in the portrait, and interior reality, as of the life. At the same time he gives the impulse to the alternating rhythm that will be the characteristic of Poe's most hallucinatory *Tales of the Grotesque and Arabesque*.

But the most singular atmosphere of the tale is lent it by the embedding of the narrator and of the narration: even the illumination of the portrait is elaborately interwoven thereby with the story of the marriage and of the two marriage beds, for the narrator becomes the second painter of the tale before Baudelaire becomes the third. The displacement and replacement of the lighting agent is intimately involved with the scene of the portrait itself, illumination and desire commingling like the gloom and grandeur of the castle enframing the entire reading. If the portrait is suddenly lit up by the beam of the candelabrum and by the gaze of the delirious reader of both texts, it was originally "thrown into deep shade by one of the bed-posts," that description already tracing a dark line from bed to painting, erotic and deadly in the same moment. The theater box of the bed is curtained, as if there too the presentation of the pictured scene were also to be a representation of the reading and interpretation, bordered in black, like the deadly double of the gilt-framed portrait. The written tale of the marriage as an unfolding of the visual text, *lying* as it does upon the very pillow of the bed, brings death for the sake of art into the bed as presumed source of life, mingles the notion of the corpse with that of creation, and makes the bed the only possible viewpoint for the tale within the tale. It is there that the text itself also expires, as if this lushly embedded tale claimed for itself an ultimate privacy, leaving no trace.

4. TRANSLATION AS OBSESSION

Baudelaire's rendering of the English text, faithful to the apparently essential, in fact blocks just the details that, upon re-reading, become significant, starting with the indications of ardent speech and deliberate closing-off, and the folding into itself of privacy. These themes intercross in their relation to the bed and the embedded portrait: "I bade Pedro to close the heavy shutters of the room—since it was already night—to light the tongues of a tall candelabrum which stood by the head of my bed, and to throw open far and wide the fringed curtains of black velvet which enveloped the bed itself." The closing of the heavy *shutters* prepares the lighting of the inflamed tongues in an expectation of some ardent word, while the pulling back of the shadowy folds that enclose the bed explicates or unfolds it, as the origin for the interpretation of what is to follow and what has passed. But none of this meaningful frame to the tale is translated into Baudelaire's version, only into his mind for a later product: the felicitous "shutters" has no French equivalent, but, more drastic, the candelabrum loses its explicit "tongues" in the other tongue, the bed, its "envelope," and almost its whole message. The passionate letter of the English text arrives in another French form altogether; the metaphor of tongues for speech as well as light is carried over to that of a tree, and mere multiplicity of nature, while the metaphors of the shutting off, of the envelope, and of the letter are changed to those of simple surrounding: "j'ordonnai à Pedro de fermer les lourds volets de la chambre—puisqu'il faisait déjà nuit—d'allumer un grand candelabre à plusieurs branches placé près de mon chevet, et d'ouvrir tout grands les rideaux de velours noir garnis de crépines qui entouraient le lit." The many tonques of fire illuminate the text as well as the reader in the English version, and the message arrives on the black-curtained scene, or in it, properly and dramatically represented. The function of the bed as matrix is scarcely to be overlooked: the insetting technique is genially increased by its staging within this embedded creation depending as much on the death of the original model as does death upon original creation. The black curtains around the bed as source for the reading crop out the inessential from the page or the wall to be read, so that "reality" is framed out and art is framed in. Yet another formal border is made here by Poe's repeated phrases focusing on focus itself, riveting the attention: "Long, long I read—and devoutly, devotedly I gazed." This first repeat and second near-repeat invite us to reread the sentence like the edge of an interior text, heavily boxed in, in an essential airlessness. Baudelaire suppresses the second repeat, a frequent omission, which lessens the heavily ornate quality of the edge: "Je lus longtemps—longtemps—je contemplai religieusement, dévotement."

This is not the only loss, or the gravest one, for in the Poe original, the interior crescendo leads to a secret suddenly wakened in the place of sleep and of creation: "At length, satisfied with the true secret of its effect, I fell back within the bed. I had found the spell of the picture in an absolute life-likeliness of expression, which, at first startling, finally confounded, subdued, and appalled me." The crescendo and the darkening of the visual text as read determine the key word here, which functions, at least in my reframing or translation of it, as the second true secret, revealed as the narrator takes a fall towards the bed of his creative interpretation in its deathly perfume. The second secret, implied in the word "appalled," mingles death—as in a pall, a pall-bearer, and to cast a pall—not over "real" life only as prediction, but also its visual semblance: "life-likeliness."

But in the Baudelaire translation, in the place of this "life-likeliness"— this term subtly expressing the very contrary of a real vitality, being artifice itself—we read another adequacy entirely, all the more appalling: "A la longue, ayant découvert le vrai secret de son effet, je me laissai retomber sur le lit. J'avais deviné que le charme de la peinture était une expression vitale absolument adéquate à la vie elle-même, qui d'abord m'avait fait tres-saillir, et finalement m'avait confondu, subjugé, épouvanté." The "vrai se-cret" of this translation or reframing is, I think, that the gentleman protests too much in attempting to reassure us about the adequation of the terms in the first representation: the adequacy replaces the life. Moreover, the im-pressive prediction of the pall of death disappears in the final word of the French frame, as "épouvanté" in the place of the key term "appalled" sup-presses the entire and double sense both of "pall" and also of the "pale" implicit there, exactly what the picture becomes in its fading, the model in her dying, the Poe text in its framing. We have only to examine some criticism about the term "appalled" in Blake's poem "London" to perceive that this word already carries in itself a long shadow, not a shade of which is to be found in the translation either of that first portrait or of its second or narrative frame.

It is, says Poe, in closing the eyes that the gaze learns to veil over and frame out what is irrelevant. Poe's "more sober and more certain gaze," however, implies only the subduing of the fancy, and a steadying of the look; the latter seems to have absorbed a veritable drunkenness in its sug-gestion, as it is contrasted with Baudelaire's narrator's gaze, "plus froide et plus sûre." The latter expression suggests not just sober, as the opposite of the poetic drunkenness to which he so often exhorts us, but also the strong feeling of "cold" as an opposition for the delirious ardor to be found in Poe's characterization of the artist's fervor communicated to the narrator. The cold is in Baudelaire quite as surely a displacement of the rigors of death found towards the beginning of the story. Here, by substitution, the proper sense is of the "pall" in "appalled," now restored.

And in this exact moment the narrator or first reader of the visual and verbal texts replaces the candelabrum, turning towards the written com-mentary on the portraits as it awaits him on his pillow. The perspective and lighting change; in Poe, the words framing this all-important turn of the text are stressed in the exact repetition of "long, long" and the "devoutly, de-votedly" quasi-repetition, insistent meditation, serving as verbal markings of the act of reading, and border words to focus the gaze. The parallel acts

of generation and degeneration in the inside story call for somber searchlights
to isolate the subject or model and to direct the look upon the darkest edge
of closure: "With deep and reverent awe I replaced the candelabrum in its
former position. The cause of my deep agitation being thus shut from view."
Here the translation conveys, surprisingly, no shutting out, but rather a
concealment or a burial at a great depth: for "shut," Baudelaire simply uses
a term for taking away or hiding, "dérobé," losing the sense of closure
and replacing the narrator as an agent of the act of hiding, an agency Poe
had deliberately transferred to the candelabrum itself ("being shut from
my view"), thus separating the cause of closure from the awe of the spectator. Baudelaire's "terreur" gives a darker color to the awe: "Avec une
terreur profonde et respectueuse, je replaçais le candelabre dans sa position première. . . . Ayant ainsi dérobé à ma vue la cause de ma profonde
agitation."

Now there are in the original two gestures of closure, first, the removal
of the source of light, second, the closing of the eyelids: both shuttings-out
or croppings-off work like a severe excluding frame, for clearer inner sight.
The English version—original, but re-read now as itself a version—accen-
tuates the closure heavily by a triple use of the terse and striking term "shut"
in a brief space of text: "while my lids remained thus shut, I ran over in my
mind my reason for so shutting them. . . . The cause of my deep agitation
being thus shut from view, I sought. . . ." The equilibrium thus established
between the monosyllabic brevity and the initial as well as the terminal
alliteration of "shut" and of "sought" stresses, quite like the regularity of
some decorative border for a picture, some exotic entwining of a serpentine
figure **S**, this closure of the text swinging upon its own mortal gates, whereas
in the translation, the repetition is rendered totally invisible by the double
avoidance of the one identical word in English. The "shut" is, as it were,
shut away: "Mais, pendant que mes paupières restaient closes, j'analysai
rapidement la raison qui me les faisait fermer ainsi. . . . Ayant ainsi dérobé
à ma vue la cause de ma profonde agitation, je cherchai. . . ."

As the light is now replaced where it had been at the start of the tale,
its beam removed from the portrait like a blinding of the canvas, the transferred illumination opens the textual or second portrait while closing off the
"real" or painted original copy of the model: life is brought to the word and
death to the lifelike image upon the wall, the most living thing about the
once-living maiden, become the bride only of art. Poe's setting exudes mor-
bidity: "the light dripped upon the pale canvas . . . the light which fell so
ghastlily . . . ," as if dripping blood, lugubrious and slow, upon the pale
canvas, marking yet again the bridal pall and pallor as the exact opposite of

the "normal" maidenly blush. The lack of this suggestion in the translation marks an emptiness in the text, not unlike the other murder committed by art; for in the French, the dripping ("s'égoutter," had Baudelaire so wished) becomes a simple filter, liquid but without the color, both the life and the menace of the English: "la lumière filtrait sur la pâle toile. . . ." The original force itself pales, but the painter and the narratee also choose not to see the pall of the genial narration, hiding what it purports to reveal.

The repetition of the refusal of the painter—"so that he *would* not see that the light which fell so ghastily. . . . And he *would* not see that the tints . . ."—as an open confession of the willful blindness, is rendered double in the second version, couched in the bed of the French. The framing repetitions of the central murder, in both the tale and the rendition, are stressed still more by the double echo of the "light which fell so ghastlily" and the end, juxtaposing the pale and the ghastly "he grew tremulous and very pallid, and aghast," which sets off the final cry, "This is indeed *Life* itself," just at the moment when the text will close upon the words "She was dead!" for a final frame, bordering in contrast and in finality what the painter's brush has sketched. From the beginning, after all, the young bride is pictured as "dreading only the pallet and brushes and other untoward instruments which deprived her of the countenance of her lover." Here already are the pall and the brush of the wing of death, with the deprivation of life assumed in that of love: from these untoward instruments the deadly portrait in its present appalling "reality" (this is "Life" itself) is made, draining the once-true colors of the past for the future fiction.

The ardent and perverse pleasure taken by painter and poet in their own reading, which recreates death in creating the work, motivates not only the replacement of the candelabrum but also of the *tongues* that might have said too much by the mortal and deadly brush. The colors dripping upon this work are drawn from the girl's features, *drawn* as the reader draws the curtains back or around his book, drawn, as one's features are drawn by sickness, drawn, finally, as a secret sense is drawn from the neutral vocabulary of a translation, already or then, as blood is drawn, for the features of another portrait of a phantom that will itself in turn be drawn from this very portrait and its life, into *life-likeliness.*

These concluding touches given to the portrait touch up at the same time the linguistic and repeating pattern within the frame: "one brush upon the mouth and one tint upon the eye . . . the brush was given, and then the tint was placed." Already the portrait is mortuary in kind, captioned by the word "brush," as if the wing of death were to brush repeatedly before our eyes. And before this deathly gaze, the spirit that first haunted the purloined text, "very spirited" as it was, trembles: "her spirit again flickered up as the flame within the socket of the lamp"; "l'esprit de la dame palpita, encore comme la flamme dans le bec d'une lampe."

Not only does the original return us to the triumphal paintings of the ghosts, those future phantoms, but the flame in its own ardor adds to the cold look of the narrator/narratee of the French version a retrospective passion. The third mortal allusion bears a still longer shadow, within the word "socket," which goes far past the signifying system of the lamp, however bright to remind the Anglo-Saxon reader, whether he will or no, of the eye, especially of the socket of the eye of a corpse. This eye that wanted to close and to be closed—like Poe's old man's eye in *The Tell-Tale Heart*, already glimpsed—has opened, and the tongues that it tried to replace have begun to murmur once more, and the shadow that he wanted to negate casts its obscurity upon the final, inescapable lucidity: "he grew very pallid." How much stronger is that than the simple "il devint très pâle" of the French, precisely by the expression to which the expression returns us: "pallid as a . . . corpse." Here at last is the phantomatic spirit of the word "appall," closing off the text and the gaze, in this brusque turn: "He turned suddenly to regard his beloved. . . ." This final gaze kills with certainty and love, like the look cast by Orpheus upon his wife: "*She was dead!*"

Death or the dead figure is found exactly at the center of the center of the egg as the image of renaissance borne implicitly by the oval portrait, so carefully framed in its repeating and opposed patterns. Far from the "real life" or the life-likeliness, it comes nearer to the "true secret" within, like the equally morbid secret of "The Oblong Box," this tale's mirror image.

5. RECUPERATION AND REFRAMING

A remarkable story is told by Baudelaire's translation of Poe's "Oval Portrait," that deeply inset history of a painter draining the life-blood of his bride to render her living picture upon the wall, the picture so passionately perceived by the narrator from his black-curtained bed on whose pillow the story lies and from which there is no exit. Baudelaire's version itself drains the blood of the ironically bedtime story to engender and embed in his own poetry two years later the second act of this heavily-framed drama of dying-into-life-as-art. His poem *Un Fantôme* explicitly includes its own frame, "Le Cadre," wherein the four parts function like the four corners of the frame for the larger picture. Between the two points, Poe's tale and the tale recounted from Poe by Baudelaire, we have seen a detectable slippage, genial and textually productive: the reframing or translating process works toward a positive end, in spite of the subject on which the texts focus (the death of the living model for the life of art). What is lost in the translation of the tale seems to be recuperated in the poem as the return of the "phantom." Baudelaire creates *Un Fantôme* quite as Poe creates the tale, and both already imitate the creation-as-murder topos of the framed topic: the intensity of the look is creative as it is macabre, and Baudelaire's recreation doubly so. The rectangular frame as coffin is implied, like another sort of "Oblong Box," with its form highly worked. This is, on the part of Baudelaire, a literary borrowing, we might say euphemistically, for what is, consciously or not, a sort of purloined letter, or just a Big Steal.

In this perspective, with the shift of this other candelabrum, we begin to re-read the paintings that Poe calls "very spirited," marvelling at Baudelaire's devivifying rendering: "pleines de style" or full of style. Styled, indeed, but it is simultaneously the elimination of Poe's strong and deliberately significant expression "highly spirited" in all its ambivalence. This was to prepare the despiriting of the actual maiden, and its own despiriting prepares instead the inspiriting of Baudelaire's own Phantom, somber and luminous, like some incarnation of an oxymoronic baroque figure in its "dazzling darkness." The Moorish frame is replaced around the Creole Jeanne, who was at the time of Baudelaire's writing of *Un Fantôme* an invalid, so that her presence in memory is all the more voluptuous for its lack of actual presence. When Baudelaire remodels the text, the spirit echoed in Poe's words will hover over the text as the eventual denial of life and over his poem, born from the difference between the original text and its rendering, in the bed of the spectator-reader, as on the later page.

The poem, now including the phantom, will absorb the Moorish frame within its model and within its own luxurious framework, keeping the pale tints, half-effaced by the wing of time, and applying them to a bedding of satin and lace, not unlike a winding sheet. Baudelaire will recuperate the textual difference in his translation and the original in order to revivify a ghostly portrait, in a literary vampirism that needs no conscious gaze to stand aghast: he too "would not see that the light which fell so ghastlily in that lone turret withered the health and the spirits of his bride. . . ." This second erotic brush, creative and murderous, of the translator's pen and the poet's own desire, stealing in order to live, makes a plumed pennant to sign away the "life-likeliness" of its model, within the curtains framing the embedded sight. If the initial glance of the late-come reader is drawn first to the portrait of life as death, it may end by perceiving in the oval frame the possibility of an egg-shaped rebirth, at least of a spirit, in the life of the poem:

XXXVIII

UN FANTÔME

I
LES TÉNÈBRES

Dans les caveaux d'insondable tristesse
Où le Destin m'a déjà relégué;
Où jamais n'entre un rayon rose et gai;
Où, seul avec la Nuit, maussade hôtesse,

Je suis comme un peintre qu'un Dieu moqueur
Condamne à peindre, hélas! sur les ténèbres;
Où, cuisinier aux appétits funèbres,
Je fais bouillir et je mange mon coeur,

Par instants brille, et s'allonge, et s'étale
Un spectre fait de grâce et de splendeur.
A sa rêveuse allure orientale,

Quand il atteint sa totale grandeur,
Je reconnais ma belle visiteuse:
C'est Elle! noire et pourtant lumineuse.

A PHANTOM

1
THE SHADOWS

Dejection has its catacombs
to which Fate has abandoned me;
no light comes, and I am left
with Night, a sullen cell-mate—

as if a scoffing God had forced
my hand to fresco . . . silhouettes!
Here with grisly appetite
I grill and devour my heart,

but then a shape looms, shining,
and as it moves it modifies:
a lovely . . . something—is there not

all the East in its easy way?
I know my visitor! *She* comes,
black—yet how that blackness glows!

II
LE PARFUM

Lecteur, as-tu quelquefois respiré
Avec ivresse et lente gourmandise
Ce grain d'encens qui remplit une église,
Ou d'un sachet le musc invétéré?

Charme profond, magique, dont nous grise
Dans le présent le passé restauré!
Ainsi l'amant sur un corps adoré
Du souvenir cueille la fleur exquise.

De ses cheveux élastiques et lourds,
Vivant sachet, encensoir de l'alcôve,
Une senteur montait, sauvage et fauve,

Et des habits, mousseline ou velours,
Tout imprégnés de sa jeunesse pure,
Se dégageait un parfum de fourrure.

2
THE PERFUME

Reader, you know how a church can reek
from one grain of incense you inhale
with careful greed—remember the smell?
Or the stubborn musk of an old sachet?

The spell is cast, the magic works,
and the present is the past—restored!
So a lover from beloved flesh
plucks subtle flowers of memory . . .

In bed her heavy resilient hair
—a living censer, like a sachet—
released its animal perfume,

and from discarded underclothes
still fervent with her sacred body's
form, there rose a scent of fur.

III
LE CADRE

Comme un beau cadre ajoute à la peinture,
Bien qu'elle soit d'un pinceau très-vanté,
Je ne sais quoi d'étrange et d'enchanté
En l'isolant de l'immense nature,

Ainsi bijoux, meubles, métaux, dorure,
S'adaptaient juste à sa rare beauté;
Rien n'offusquait sa parfaite clarté,
Et tout semblait lui servir de bordure.

Même on eût dit parfois qu'elle croyait
Que tout voulait l'aimer; elle noyait
Sa nudité voluptueusement

Dans les baisers du satin et du linge,
Et, lente ou brusque, à chaque mouvement
Montrait la grâce enfantine du singe.

3
THE FRAME

As the fine frame completes a canvas
(even one from a master's hand),
adding an indefinable magic
by dividing art from mere nature,

so jewels, mirrors, metals, gold
invariably suited her loveliness—
none violated the lustre she had,
and each thing seemed to set her off.

You might have said, sometimes, she thought
objects longed to make love to her,
so greedily she slaked her nakedness

on the kisses of linen sheets and silk,
revealing with each movement all
the unstudied grace of a marmoset.

IV

LE PORTRAIT

La Maladie et la Mort font des cendres
De tout le feu qui pour nous flamboya.
De ces grands yeux si fervents et si tendres,
De cette bouche où mon coeur se noya,

De ces baisers puissants comme un dictame,
De ces transports plus vifs que des rayons,
Que reste-t-il? C'est affreux, ô mon âme!
Rien qu'un dessin fort pâle, aux trois crayons,

Qui, comme moi, meurt dans la solitude,
Et que le Temps, injurieux vieillard,
Chaque jour frotte avec son aile rude . . .

Noir assassin de la Vie et de l'Art,
Tu ne tueras jamais dans ma mémoire
Celle qui fut mon plaisir et ma gloire!

4

THE PORTRAIT

Look what Death and Disease have made
of our old flame: a heap of ashes.
My god, how horrible! What's left
of eyes so soft yet so intense,

of kisses stronger than any drug,
of a mouth that used to drown my heart,
of all our glowing exaltation?
Precious little—barely a sketch

fading in a solitude like mine,
erased a little more each day
by disrespectful Time that wipes

out Life and Art; yet even Time
cannot force me to forget Her
who was my glory and my Joy!
                    (Richard Howard, trans.)

Baudelaire's *Un Fantôme* may be seen now as a double ghost, already coming back in two stages, in the poem itself explicitly, and then coming from the remains of the Poe story implicitly, thus, framed within that story in its French rendering. It is, like the original story, inserted and buried right at the beginning within a somber niche, within "caves of unfathomable sadness," where the canvas of the poet-as-painter is composed solely of shadows. The gloomy hostess prepares for this new cave man a collation exactly appropriate to funebral appetites: the dark background of the painting in "Les Ténèbres" is stretched out horizontally like a black tablecloth to receive the macabre feast of boiled heart, that traditional romantic dish of poets: "he will eat out his heart." The painting prepared for the self by fate as the hostess, but also self-prepared: "I am like a painter," is to be read as black on black, the gruesome dish preparing the mortal fading from one sonnet to the next in the four sections where life seeps away, and the verbs progressively lose their energy:

manger

respirer

regarder

mourir

From the initial dark caverns to the alcove and the altar of "Le Portrait" and its erotic secret places, like some amatory church where the censer shakes out the heavy fragrance ("Le Parfum") upon a perfumed fur, "Le Parfum" is itself protected by a heavy frame as ornate as the Moorish one of Poe's own making. The poem, like the portrait, is bordered in filigree, at once to isolate the scene in sanctity for the ritual worship and to ensure the private value. The exquisite black flower will bloom only once in this place to set aside, in this radiance so ephemeral where "pure youth" in all its paradoxical lush secrecy will have quickly perished amid the deep velvet and upon the redolent fur so outspread as on some couch, this rebedding blasphemously and wonderfully lit by a torch, as by the former candelabrum, near the alter of a wild passion. It is just this outspoken and secret contrariness that gives this portrait its feverish exaltation, in these stanzas, like the model, at once "black and luminous." The model herself is dressed in contraries, both in the pure muslin of youthful innocence and in the deeply dark velvet plushness of the siren, a costumed incorporation of the heaven-and-hell double postulation characteristic of Baudelaire. The model's figure, reeling with the dizzying incense and the intoxication of desire, will sink gradually into a deadly calm in the imperfect tense, drenched in satin kisses: all this within the framework of the third part upon which the gaze is concentrated by its explicit Frame. The key words here included are the once again opposed "kiss" and "drowning," amatory and morbid, recurring in the last part of "The Portrait," to take on there a negative sense. The identification of love with death is intensified in this moment, before this altar for synesthesia, in both senses of the senses, so that death is reframed and retouched—touched up as a painting is touched up, or as death touches up the colors of life— toward this re-reading that summons us, as toward an altar: "Lecteur, as-tu quelquefois. . . ." Such repetitions form part of this frame that adds to painting, often mortal as it is human.

"Le Cadre" of the third part now surrounds the painting with its strangeness, setting apart the model from the actual mistress, bedecked in fittings precious yet peculiar. This isolated space retains the richly valued image jealously guarded among the treasures thrown in a heap: "jewels, furniture, metals, gilt," everything together as if Poe's "Philosophy of Furniture" were to cast an odd light upon this former "perfect clarity," placed from the beginning against a shadowy backdrop, deadly in its infolding or implication. As she is bordered or edged in by the frame, within her gilded couch, the shadow of another verb, "bordée" or tucked in, adds for the obsessed reader the hint of another bedding altogether. With the "very celebrated" brush of painter and poet, the intense voluptuousness of the painting takes no verbal embroidery, no poetic jewels, for the model is sufficiently bedecked and bejewelled as she is embedded in the poem.

After the altar of passion inflamed and ablaze against the shadows and the frame as of gold around a madonna, set around the picture, this last section of "Le Portrait" portrays a night and death-watch at the bed of Love's prisoner, who will be the prisoner of Death as soon as her portrait is finished. The blaze dies down to ashes, as the reversal is made: the one who was, says the painter, "my pleasure and my glory" will bring death to the painter himself. Like the loving husband-artist with his brush in the Poe story, the poet-artist devours his model for his art and kills himself in turn with the sacrifice of his love. The flowering love for the model-mistress will be cut off in order to nourish the life of the art-in-flower, that is, transformed into a memory before its own altar. The model wins out over the woman, and the poet-artist over the lover-husband, as the heavy baroque colors, black and red and gold, become less vivid in this three-colored pale sketch, "ce dessin fort pâle, aux trois crayons," as if the three spindles of the fates were to have replaced the unique and famed brush of the painter, instilling not just a pastel but a deathly pallor. The painter will be remembered for his celebrated and secret portrait of this model, who came here upon the scene as a black and luminous visitor, a phantom from another highly spirited text, already a spectre, to remain as an effigy. In this other "Harmonie du soir" with its censer, its altar, and its monstrance, all wrapped in a vertiginous perfumed spell of twilight, the initial pleasure gives way to death, and death to memory in its isolated performance set in the borders of ritual and in the frame of art.

6. ADDITION AS SUBTRACTION

The paradox is terrible in what it so clearly implies: indeed, the frame adds to the painting, but by setting it apart and, finally, by killing its model. This isolation of the third part of Baudelaire's picture, where the Frame is openly the entitled subject, is, in the fourth part or Portrait itself in summation, the gravest of solitudes, where death does its own framing in the greatest possible bareness of design. To preserve her from death, the painter or poet, the one always as the other now, circumscribes the model by "life-like" artifice, but the vital lines that stretch from the real woman to the surroundings are cropped off, exactly as curtains are pulled back so that the drama may be seen, or then the curtains around the couch of dream and narration so that the tale may be recounted. What the passionate glance of the artist-in-love obscures by its very ardor, as of a dazzling darkness penetrating the very core of life as art, is the fact that these presentational curtains stifle the movements of the reader so *embedded* in the narration just as surely as the ornate frame stifles the model so enframed in the picture, cutting her off from the flux of life itself. So outlined, so lifelike-seeming, the severed object perishes.

The "beau cadre" adding its funereal edges to protect the beauty of the living portrait of this new and dark Venus checks any movement of the model, thus rigidly fixed in her limits at once enchanted and nonetheless normal (the mistress of the poet or artist is, after all, the model by rights). Before the painter's gaze and that of the narrator of the double canvas, both visual and textual, and then before that of Baudelaire as the second reader and all others, including ourselves, the living portrait grows pale, as she is now triply enframed. By the canvas, by the text, and by the bedding, the model in her gilt and jewels and arty finery is transfixed, impotent against the representation of the wing of time, that "aile" in language and in art arising from the very mention of herself the first time, "Elle," and in the very moment when the poet and the painter (ironically in the case of Baude-laire, the celebrator of "the painter of modern life") is putting his mortal last touches on the exquisite flower imprisoned in her luxurious frame. Of all this black and luminous radiance there will remain only the perfumed memory and her halo in the secretly illuminated niche for a saint more voluptuous than saintly, whose brilliance dies within this poem. Circumspection, or the roundabout gaze, leads for the reader and writer as for the poet and painter to circumscription, or writing around this framing outline; so the look cast upon the translation itself has permitted a longer look at a supplemental study of the experiment of translation as frame, and as final frame-up.

7. OBLIQUE GAZE

A year after *Les Fleurs du Mal* appears Baudelaire's translation of the *Narrative of Arthur Gordon Pym*, whose preface bears a warning about the difficulty of writing an account of adventures that would be "so minute and connected as to have the *appearance* of that truth it would really possess." But in French the statement is a different one: "pour avoir toute la physionomie de la vérité—dont il serait cependant l'expression réelle." Now by the altered terms "physionomie" and "expression" we are kept in the realm of the portrait, Baudelaire's continual obsession, whereas in the original, there is no trace of a portrait, just of an appearance, and then, of the truth of the possession. In fact, the balance between seeming and having is the focus of these linguistic adventures, subsequent to the other adventures that they retrospectively frame.

If we turn our attention to the portrait of the artist himself, Baudelaire's pen attributes, or seems to attribute, the preface to Arthur Gordon Pym, assuring us we will have not the slightest difficulty in seeing where the few pages of his tale written by Mr. Poe give way to his own tale, and his own voice: "it will be unnecessary to point out where his portion ends and my own commences; the difference in point of style will be readily perceived." That suffices to complicate the relations between appearance and real physiognomy: more than a stylistic difference is at stake. From Poe's style, "serré et concaténé" as Baudelaire describes it, tightened as in a vice, closely linked as in a concentrated space, as in a frame, Baudelaire makes a better tale than any other translator could, for in this interlacing of two faces and physiognomy and of two voices and two gazes, the loss and the profit will bear progeny.

From the incipit-as-lie ("My name is Arthur Gordon Pym") and its exact double, doubly a lie ("Mon nom est Arthur Gordon Pym") until the inconclusive conclusion, two or three chapters are lost—so we are told—and the tale is in lack. To discover the true text, then, we should perhaps follow the same procedure as the narrator-adventurer; holed up in his hiding-place, or "in the hold" of another force, within another space than the normal one to which we are assigned. His effort to read the little slip of paper as message is successful only when his gaze makes itself oblique, when he sees it *askance;* it is, moreover, a gaze reversed, for the written words give him, precisely, the *slip,* when he neglects to look at the other side: "the other, or under side, then, was that on which lay the writing, if writing there should finally prove to be." When, in the light of the phosphorous, he reads the seven concluding words, "blood—your life depends upon lying close," he learns what we learn as readers: to be possessed, "to lie close," suggesting already the embrace of something or someone supposing already an erotic sense, and possession itself, in some obsessive "hold" or "grip" we should not loose. This is the major lesson of a passionate reading.

But in the Baudelaire version, it is a matter simply of lying hidden in one's hiding place; the original is indeed in its hiding place within the French version: "sang—restez caché, votre vie en dépend." All the terms of the original document, those terms on which, I think, we should take the text, focus on the same subject, that of possession—that subject is what my text means to frame. That is what seclusion imposes, remaining hidden within that other face of Poe's own painting, and life drains from it to nourish something else. That physiognomy perceived in Baudelaire's version is precisely not "l'expression réelle," that *expression* itself invented by Baudelaire; that lack and that lie are the source for still another possession, that of this reading by that second text.

If the Baudelairean grip on the English-language reader takes hold of us in fact, it is in the fashion of the *incitamentum* or the little detail that incites Poe to discover his own *incipit.* A wonderful set of teeth, for instance, as in *Bérénice;* there again we fell the hold and the bite, quite like that of the dog menacing the narrator in Pym: the *incitamentum* could be defined as something that grabs you in its teeth, getting a grip upon you—circumscription with a vengeance.

As the narrator, like the narrator-reader of "The Oval Portrait," incites us to read also this fragment "slightly askance," let the reader re-read this text of possession and erotic deciphering: when the lost fragment of the tale is juxtaposed with the other text, this bloody bit scratched and scribbled in red will urge the substance from its ink, the red trace italicized from its tale: "*I have scrawled this with blood—your life depends upon lying close.*" And that continues to remain hidden in the Baudelairean hold taken of the matter, life having passed into the other text.

Might not the possessive embrace of the hide-out and the reader—"the hold it has over him"—return us to the bed of the narrator-reader of "The Oval Portrait," like a theater box surrounded with black velvet curtains, which we might, were our imagination ardent enough, see now as red? Might this embedded reading as imitation, yielding the painting with its traits stolen from life, itself be read as a double transformation of the Dracula legend, as a bloody and textual execution in the flicking light of the candles with their "tongues" of flame well hidden by the cover of the second tongue? If these two tales took proper possession of the spirit of the reader, as it is impaired and embraced, might the weakened narrator framed within his own curtains not be seen to suffer the same fate as the girl whose virgin blood is drawn by the monster, in a scene where it would be impossible to distinguish one from the other bed-ridden desire? Sickness, transfusion of blood and of tongues, baroque intertwining of life and art, of death and love: as Baudelaire points out, all Poe's arrows "fly toward the same end." They obey the language of submission and love; pens and feathers—as in the double sense of *plume*—have been seen to fly also, sometimes for the benefit of the reader, in the embedded hideout. The portrait of Poe is set by Baudelaire, within a new oval frame: this strange embrace is productive, for the egg of the oval is hatched within. But the text, like the slip of paper, can only be read askance: the oval leaves room for an imperfect form of reading, not a circle, but an ellipsis, when the reading itself is forced to become elliptical, circumspect like the circumscription.

There follows then the period of gestation and disguise-as-death: the narrator, taking on the physiognomy of death, looks at himself only in a fragment of mirror, to mirror the preceding fragments of text. All the arrows continue to fly toward the same goal: disguise, fragment, looks set aslant, elliptical reading. The episode of the mysterious ship contains its own reserve of sense, its hidden meaning. How could we know without comparing the two versions what the following sentence hides beneath its apparent simplicity: "Le navire en vue était un grand brick-goelette?" For the translation has once more effaced the key term, covering it over or rather translating it into a different form: "The vessel in sight was a large hermaphrodite brig." The black steamer with its figurehead gilded and highly visible is thus the bearer of a heavy meaning, like the haunting embrace of two unlike forms within a key figure. The French version translates the embrace of male with female term, but once more the underlying female figure is at least partially effaced, wiped out, in the portrait of the phantom ship, pictured between black borders tinted with gold. The appearance of the object focused upon is once again assured, as was the "life-likeliness" of that other portrait, to the end: "I relate these things and circumstances minutely, and I relate them, it must be understood, precisely as they *appeared* to us."

The appearance embraces and hides: the enormous seagull devouring the face of the man on board until only his set of very white teeth appears in view, inciting, like the teeth of the cadaver in *Bérénice*, to wonder—the toothy sparkle strikes the sight just as it is perceived that the eyes above them are pecked out. At this point the tongue ceases to recount ("this the— but I forbear") like a dead tongue: "And the hue *of* the skin *of* the figure was *of* the perfect whiteness *of* the snow." Here the figure is shrouded, and circumspect, whereas the French stops short, as if from a dead man's tongue: "mais je m'arrête."

The place is red, but all trace of blood will disappear from the conclusion, which carries a sign of lack: the original closes by the repetition of the segments of a measured sentence, marking the solemn blows as if to salute the apparition of a great human figure, *shrouded* as if in death, whereas in the second version, the French reader sees only a "veiled" form where the winding-sheet remains unspoken. The mortuary shadows disappear, and the sentence ends only with three dots, suspending the sight in the snow: "Et la couleur de la peau de l'homme était la blancheur parfaite de la neige. . . ." Unlike the curtaining by death in "The Oval Portrait," this opening remains gaping in the snow, leaving exposed against and upon the white background the odd lyricism of the white letter inscribed, opposed to the shadowy being, in a baroque opposition from which, however, the red has disappeared, leaving only white and dark. Inscriptions mark the mind, like the mysterious pattern in the labyrinth of what might be read as an encoded *aile* or *Elle*. Inset into the text that frames it, the figure encircles a womb-like space, as if to embed some secret:

Fig. I.

The final "sinuosities" close the text over its own inscription traced in the dust and the rock inscribed as a response to the blood-red text previously scrawled on or engraved in the *slip* of paper that may cross the reader's mind from time to time. The original closes upon its own *windings*, sinuous, to be sure, but spiraling also about other gestures, as in the winding up of a clock, or a tale, completing the haunting system of hiding-place, embrace, and embedded reading, passions in the final dust, where every trace of blood, as the basic sign of life, has disappeared as in the shadowy background of some monumental and murderous frame.

8. TRANSLATION AS FRAMING

Finally, what is translated is also framed; the splendid isolation conferred upon the picture by the second brush may be penned in heavily or lightly. Genius uses what it betrays, and well: Baudelaire's supplement adds richly to our own seeing.

In that alcove that he opens for us within his dark caverns with their heavy-laden tables and their terrible feast, the focus is upon his secret painting whose goal is the restoration of the past within the present. Here the flower of a youth perfumed and perishing upon some scented fur is sensed once more, but within a black-edged frame, which has absorbed, and is absorbed within, the rich gilt frames of Moorish design. The golden halos projected about the head of painter as of poet, and the vignetting technique of his recreated Oval Portrait, whose figure can be guaranteed not to fade, take the original and lifelike obsession with a legend into a second rendering with all the added riches and the productive losses, constructing thus a double frame about the inner figure upon the wall or page. This is a work for and of passionate circumspection and circumscription and demands a response no less passionate in its look, in its text, and in its translation.

The critic is thus called upon in turn to treat the topic and the sight in a limited or circumscribed space, to insulate the incident and to add "the force of a frame to the picture," arresting the flux of reasonable reading by an ardent enclosure. Of this portrait and its end, there is perhaps no original; it might be then a picture of representation, with no model, or a model at once crimson and already pallid in its frame. As translation sets frame across from frame, and within it, so the readings and re-readings keep their odd faith with passion as with pallor.

PAUL DE MAN

Anthropomorphism and Trope
in the Lyric

The gesture that links epistemology with rhetoric in general, and not only
with the mimetic tropes of representation, recurs in many philosophical and
poetic texts of the nineteenth century, from Keats's "Beauty is truth, truth
beauty" to Nietzsche's perhaps better known than understood definition of
truth as tropological displacement: "Was ist also Wahrheit? Ein bewegliches
Heer von Metaphern, Metonymien, Anthropomorphismen. . . ." Even
when thus translated before it has been allowed to run one third of its course,
Nietzsche's sentence considerably complicates the assimilation of truth to
trope that it proclaims. Later in the essay, the homology between concept
and figure as symmetrical structures and aberrant repressions of differences is dramatized in the specular destinies of the artist and the scientist-
philosopher. Like the Third Critique, this late Kantian text demonstrates,
albeit in the mode of parody, the continuity of aesthetic with rational judgment that is the main tenet and the major crux of all critical philosophies
and "Romantic" literatures. The considerable difference in tone between
Nietzsche and Kant cannot conceal the congruity of the two projects, their
common stake in the recovery of controlled discourse on the far side of even
the sharpest denials of intuitive sense-certainties. What interests us primarily
in the poetic and philosophical versions of this transaction, in this give-and-
take between reason and imagination, is not, at this point, the critical schemes
that deny certainty considered in themselves, but their disruption by patterns
that cannot be reassimilated to these schemes, but that are nevertheless, if

From *The Rhetoric of Romanticism*. © 1984 by Columbia University Press.

not produced, then at least brought into focus by the distortions the disruption inflicts upon them.

Thus, in the Nietzsche sentence, the recovery of knowledge by ways of its devalorization in the deviance of the tropes is challenged, even at this moment of triumph for a critical reason which dares to ask and to reply to the question: what is truth? First of all, the listing of particular tropes is odd, all the more so since it is technically more precise than is often the case in such arguments: only under the pen of a classical philologist such as Nietzsche is one likely to find combined, in 1872, what Gérard Genette has since wittily referred to as the two "chiens de faience" of contemporary rhetoric—metaphor and metonymy. But the third term in the enumeration, anthropomorphism, is no longer a philological and neutral term, neither does it complement the two former ones: anthropomorphisms can contain a metaphorical as well as a metonymic moment—as in an Ovidian metamorphosis in which one can start out from the contiguity of the flower's name to that of the mythological figure in the story, or from the resemblance between a natural scene and a state of soul.

The term "anthropomorphism" therefore adds little to the two previous ones in the enumeration, nor does it constitute a synthesis between them, since neither metaphor nor metonymy have to be necessarily anthropomorphic. Perhaps Nietzsche, in the Voltairean conte philosophique *On Truth and Lie* is just being casual in his terminology—but then, opportunities to encounter technical tropological terms are so sparse in literary and philosophical writings that one can be excused for making the most of it when they occur. The definition of truth as a collection ("army" being, aside from other connotations, at any rate a collective term) of tropes is a purely structural definition, devoid of any normative emphasis; it implies that truth is relational, that it is an articulation of a subject (for example "truth") and a predicate (for example "an army of tropes") allowing for an answer to a definitional question (such as "what is truth?") that is not purely tautological. At this point, to say that truth is a trope is to say that truth is the possibility of stating a proposition; to say that truth is a collection of varied tropes is to say that it is the possibility of stating several propositions about a single subject, of relating several predicates to a subject according to principles of articulation that are not necessarily identical: truth is the possibility of definition by means of infinitely varied sets of propositions. This assertion is purely descriptive of an unchallenged grammatical possibility and, as such, it has no critical thrust, nor does it claim to have one: there is nothing inherently disruptive in the assertion that truth is a trope.

But "anthropomorphism" is not just a trope but an identification on the level of substance. It takes one entity for another and thus implies the constitution of specific entities prior to their confusion, the *taking* of something for something else that can then be assumed to be *given*. Anthropomorphism freezes the infinite chain of tropological transformations and propositions into one single assertion or essence which, as such, excludes all others. It is no longer a proposition but a proper name, as when the metamorphosis in Ovid's stories culminates and halts in the singleness of a proper name, Narcissus or Daphne or whatever. Far from being the same, tropes such as metaphor (or metonymy) and anthropomorphisms are mutually exclusive. The apparent enumeration is in fact a foreclosure which acquires, by the same token, considerable critical power.

Truth is now defined by two incompatible assertions: either truth is a set of propositions or truth is a proper name. Yet, on the other hand, it is clear that the tendency to move from tropes to systems of interpretations such as anthropomorphisms is built into the very notion of trope. One reads Nietzsche's sentence without any sense of disruption, for although a trope is in no way the same as an anthropomorphism, it is nevertheless the case that an anthropomorphism is structured like a trope: it is easy enough to cross the barrier that leads from trope to name but impossible, once this barrier has been crossed, to return from it to the starting-point in "truth." Truth is a trope; a trope generates a norm or value; this value (or ideology) is no longer true. It is true that tropes are the producers of ideologies that are no longer true.

Hence the "army" metaphor. Truth, says Nietzsche, is a mobile *army* of tropes. Mobility is coextensive with any trope, but the connotations introduced by "army" are not so obvious, for to say that truth is an army (of tropes) is again to say something odd and possibly misleading. It can certainly not imply, in *On Truth and Lie* that truth is a kind of commander who enlists tropes in the battle against error. No such dichotomy exists in any critical philosophy, let alone Nietzsche's, in which truth is always at the very least dialectical, the negative knowledge of error. Whatever truth may be fighting, it is not error but stupidity, the belief that one is right when one is in fact in the wrong. To assert, as we just did, that the assimilation of truth to tropes is not a disruption of epistemology, is not to assert that tropes are therefore true or on the side, so to speak, of truth. Tropes are neither true nor false and are both at once. To call them an army is however to imply that their effect and their effectiveness is not a matter of judgment but of power. What characterizes a good army, as distinct for instance from a good cause, is that its success has little to do with immanent justice and a great deal with the proper economic use of its power. One willingly admits that truth has power, including the power to occur, but to say that its power is like that of an army and to say this within the definitional context of the question: what is therefore truth? is truly disruptive. It not only asserts that truth (which was already complicated by having to be a proposition as well as a proper name) is also power, but a power that exists independently of epistemological determinations, although these determinations are far from being nonexistent: calling truth an army *of tropes* reaffirms its epistemological *as well as* its strategic power. How the two modes of power could exist side by side certainly baffles the mind, if not the grammar of Nietzsche's tale. The sentence that asserts the complicity of epistemology and rhetoric, of truth and trope, also turns this alliance into a battle made all the more dubious by the fact that the adversaries may not even have the opportunity ever to encounter each other. Less schematically compressed, more elaborated and dramatized instances of similar disjunctions can be found in the texts of lyrical poets, such as, for example, Baudelaire.

The canonical and programmatic sonnet "Correspondances" contains not a single sentence that is not simply declarative. Not a single negation, interrogation, or exclamation, not a single verb that is not in the present indicative, nothing but straightforward affirmation: "la Nature *est* un temple . . . Il *est* des parfums frais comme des chairs d'enfants." The least assertive word in the text is the innocuous "parfois" in line 2, hardly a dramatic temporal break. Nor is there (a rare case in *Les Fleurs du Mal*) any pronominal agitation: no *je-tu* apostrophes or dialogues, only the most objective descriptions of third persons. The only personal pronoun to appear is the impersonal "il" of "il est (des parfums). . . ."

The choice of "Correspondances" to explicate the quandaries of language as truth, as name, and as power may therefore appear paradoxical and forced. The ironies and the narrative frame of *On Truth and Lie* make it difficult to take the apparent good cheer of its tone at face value, but the serenity of "Correspondances" reaches deep enough to eliminate any disturbance of the syntactical surface. This serenity is prevalent enough to make even the question superfluous. Nietzsche still has to dramatize the summation of his story in an eyecatching paragraph that begins with the question of questions: Was ist also Wahrheit? But Baudelaire's text is all assurance and all answer. One has to make an effort to perceive the opening line as an answer to an implicit question, "La Nature est un temple . . ." as the answer to "Qu'est-ce que la nature?" The title is not "La Nature," which would signal a need for definition; in "Correspondances," among many other connotations, one hears "response," the dialogical exchange that takes place in mutual proximity to a shared entity called nature. The *response* to the sonnet, among its numerous readers and commentators, has been equally responsive. Like the oracle of Delphi, it has been made to answer a considerable number and variety of questions put to it by various readers. Some of these questions are urgent (such as: how can one be innocent and corrupt at the same time?), some more casually historical (such as: when can modern French lyric poetry, from Baudelaire to surrealism and beyond, be said to begin?). In all cases, the poem has never failed to answer to the satisfaction of its questioner.

The serenity of the diction celebrates the powers of tropes or "symboles" that can reduce any conceivable difference to a set of polarities and combine them in an endless play of substitution and amalgamation, extending from the level of signification to that of the signifier. Here, as in Nietzsche's text, the telos of the substitutions is the unified system "esprit/sens" (l. 14), the seamless articulation, by ways of language, of sensory and aesthetic experience with the intellectual assurance of affirmation. Both echo each other in the controlled compression of a brief and highly formalized sonnet which can combine the enigmatic depth of doctrine—sending commentators astray in search of esoteric authority—with the utmost banality of a phrase such as "verts comme les prairies."

On the thematic level, the success of the project can be measured by the unquestioned acceptance of a paradox such as "Vaste comme la nuit et comme la clarté," in which a conjunctive *et* can dare to substitute for what should be the *ou* of an either/or structure. For the vastness of the night is one of confusion in which distinctions disappear, Hegel's night in which $A = A$ because no such thing as A can be discerned, and in which infinity is homogeneity. Whereas the vastness of light is like the capacity of the mind to make endless analytical distinctions, or the power of calculus to integrate by ways of infinitesimal differentiation. The juxtaposition of these incompatible meanings is condensed in the semantic ambiguity of "se confondent," which can designate the bad infinity of confusion as well as the fusion of opposites into synthetic judgments. That "echoes," which are originally the disjunction of a single sensory unit or word by the alien obstacle of a reflection, themselves re-fuse into a single sound ("Comme de longs échos qui de loin se confondent") again acts out the dialectic of identity and difference, of sensory diffuseness and intellectual precision.

The process is self-consciously verbal or mediated by language, as is clear from the couple "se confondent / se répondent," which dramatizes events of discourse and in which, as was already pointed out, "se répondent" should be read as "se correspondent" rather than as a pattern of question and answer. As in "confuses paroles" and "symboles" in the opening lines, the stress on language as the stage of disjunction is unmistakable. Language can be the chain of metaphors in a synethesia, as well as the oxymoronic polysemy of a single word, such as "se confondent" (or "transports" in l. 14) or even, on the level of the signifier, the play of the syllable or the letter. For the title, "Correspondances," is like the anagrammatic condensation of the text's entire program: "corps" and "esprit" brought together and harmonized by the *ance* of assonance that pervades the concluding tercets: from *ayant, ambre, chantent* to *expansion, sens, transport,* finally redoubled and re-echoed in *enc-ens/sens.*

The assertion, or representation, of verbality in "se répondent" (or in "Laissent parfois sortir de confuses *paroles*") also coincides, as in Nietzsche's text, with the passage from tropes—here the substitution of one sense experience by another—to anthropomorphisms. Or so, at least, it seems to a perhaps overhasty reading that would at once oppose "nature" to "homme" as in a polarity of art ("temple") and nature, and endow natural forests and trees with eyes ("regards") and voices. The tradition of interpretation for this poem, which stresses the importance of Chateaubriand and of Gérard de Nerval as sources, almost unanimously moves in that direction.

The opening lines allow but certainly do not impose such a reading. "La Nature est un temple" is enigmatic enough to constitute the burden of any attempt at understanding and cannot simply be reduced to a pattern of binary substitution, but what follows is hardly less obscure. "Vivants piliers," as we first meet it, certainly suggests the erect shape of human bodies naturally enough endowed with speech, a scene from the paintings of Paul Delvaux rather than from the poems of Victor Hugo. "L'homme," in line 3, then becomes a simple apposition to "vivants piliers." The notion of nature as a wood and, consequently, of "piliers" as anthropomorphic columns and trees, is suggested only by "des *forêts* de symboles" in which, especially in combination with "symboles," a natural and descriptive reading of "forêt" is by no means compelling. Nor is nature, in Baudelaire, necessarily a sylvan world. We cannot be certain whether we have ever left the world of humans and whether it is therefore relevant or necessary to speak of anthropomorphism at all in order to account for the figuration of the text. "Des forêts," a plural of what is already, in the singular, a collective plural (forêt) can be read as equivalent to "une foule de symboles," a figure of amplification that designates a large number, the crowd of humanity in which it is well known that Baudelaire took a constant poetic, rather than humanitarian, interest.

Perhaps we are not in the country at all but have never left the city, the "rue assourdissante" of the poem entitled "A une passante," for example. "Symboles" in "des forêts de symboles" could then designate the verbal, the

rhetorical dimension within which we constantly dwell and which we therefore meet as passively as we meet the glance of the other in the street. That
the possibility of this reading seems farfetched and, in my experience, never
fails to elicit resistance, or that the forest/temple cliché should have forced
itself so emphatically upon the attention of the commentators is one of the
cruxes of "Correspondances."

It has been enough of a crux for Baudelaire himself to have generated
at least one other text, the poem "Obsession," to which we will have to turn
later. For the possibility of anthropomorphic (mis)reading is part of the text
and part of what is at stake in it. Anthropomorphism seems to be the illu-
sionary resuscitation of the natural breath of language, frozen into stone by
the semantic power of the trope. It is a figural affirmation that claims to
overcome the deadly negative power invested in the figure. In Baudelaire's,
as in Nietzsche's text, the icon of this central trope is that of the architectural
construct, temple, beehive, or columbarium.

This verbal building, which has to celebrate at the same time funeral
and rebirth, is built by the infinite multiplication of numbers raising each
other to ever higher arithmetic power. The property which privileges "parfums" as the sensory analogon for the joint powers of mind and body (ll.
9–14) is its ability to grow from the infinitely small to endless expansion,
"ce grain d'encens qui remplit une église"—a quotation from *Les Fleurs de
Mal* that made it into Littré. The religious connotation of "temple" and
"encens" suggests, as in the immediately anterior poem in the volume, "Elé-
vation," a transcendental circulation, as ascent or descent, between the spirit
and the senses, a borderline between two distinct realms that can be crossed.

Yet this movement is not unambiguously sustained by all the articu-
lations of the text. Thus in the line "L'homme y passe à travers des forêts
de symboles," "passer à travers" can have two very different spatial meanings.
It can read as "traverser la forêt"; one can *cross* the woods, as Narcissus goes
through the looking-glass, or as the acrobat, in Banville's poem that echoes
in Mallarmé's "Le Pitre châtié," goes through the roof of the circus tent, or
as Vergil, for that matter, takes Dante beyond the woods in which he lost
his way. But "passer à travers" can also mean to remain enclosed in the
wood, to wander and err around in it as the speaker of "A une passante"
wanders around in the crowd. The latter reading in fact suits the represented
scene better than the former, although it is incompatible with the transcendental claims usually made for the sonnet. The transcendence of substitutive,
analogical tropes linked by the recurrent "comme," a transcendence which
occurs in the declarative assurance of the first quatrain, states the totalizing
power of metaphor as it moves from analogy to identity, from simile to

symbol and to a higher order of truth. Ambivalences such as those noted in
"passer à travers," as well as the theoretical ambivalence of anthropomorphism in relation to tropes, complicate this expectation perhaps more forcefully than its outright negation. The complication is forceful enough to
contaminate the key word that carries out the substitutions which constitute
the main structure of the text: the word "comme."

When it is said the "Les parfums, les couleurs et les sons se répondent
. . . *comme* de longs échos," than the preposition of resemblance, "comme,"
the most frequently counted word in the canon of Baudelaire's poetry, does
its work properly and clearly, without upsetting the balance between difference and identity that it is assigned to maintain. It achieves a figure of
speech, for it is not actually the case that an answer is an echo; no echo has
ever answered a question except by a "delusion" of the signifier—but it is
certainly the case that an echo sounds like an answer, and that this similarity
is endlessly suggestive. And the catachresis "se répondent" to designate the
association between the various senses duly raises the process to the desired
higher power. "Des parfums . . . / Doux comme les hautbois, verts comme
les prairies" is already somewhat more complex, for although it is possible
in referential and semantic terms to think of oboes and of certain scents as
primarily "soft," it makes less sense to think of scents as green: "green scents"
have less compelling connotations than "green thoughts" or "green shades."
The relaying "comme" travels by ways of "hautbois," solidly tied to "parfums" by ways of "doux" and altogether compatible with "vert," through
the pastoral association of the reedy sound still reinforced by the "(haut)*bois*,
verts" that would be lost in English or German translation. The greenness
of the fields can be guided back from color to scent with any "unsweet"
connotation carefully filtered out.

All this is playing at metaphor according to the rules of the game. But
the same is not true of the final "comme" in the poem: "Il est des parfums
frais comme . . . / Doux comme . . . / —Et d'autres . . . / Ayant l'expansion
des choses infinies / *Comme* l'ambre, le musc, le benjoin et l'encens." Ce
comme n'est pas un comme comme les autres. It does not cross from one
sense experience to another, as "frais" crosses from scent to touch or "doux"
from scent to sound, nor does it cross from the common sensorium back to
the single sense of hearing (as in "Les parfums, les couleurs et les sons se
répondent" "Comme de longs échos . . .") or from the sensory to the intellectual realm, as in the double register of "se confondent." In each of these
cases, the "comme" is what avoids tautology by linking the subject to a
predicate that is not the same: scents are said to be like oboes, or like fields,
or like echoes. But here "comme" relates to the subject "parfums" in two

different ways or, rather, it has two distinct subjects. If "comme" is related to "l'expansion des choses infinies," which is grammatically as well as tonally possible, then it still functions, like the other "commes," as a comparative simile: a common property ("l'expansion") links the finite senses to an experience of infinity. But "comme" also relates to "parfums": Il est des parfums frais . . . / —Et d'autres . . . / Comme l'ambre, le musc, le benjoin et l'encens"; the somewhat enigmatic hyphen can be said to mark that hesitation (as well as rule it out). "Comme" then means as much as "such as, for example" and enumerates scents which contrast with "chairs d'enfants" as innocence contrasts with experience or nature with artifice. This working out by exemplification is quite different from the analogical function assigned to the other uses of "comme."

Considered from the perspective of the "thesis" or of the symbolist ideology of the text, such a use of "comme" is aberrant. For although the burden of totalizing expansion seems to be attribute to these particular scents rather than the others, the logic of "comme" restricts the semantic field of "parfums" and confines it to a tautology: "Il est des parfums . . . / Comme (des parfums)." Instead of analogy, we have enumeration, and an enumeration which never moves beyond the confines of a set of particulars: "forêt" synthesizes but does not enumerate a set of trees, but "ambre," "musc," "benjoin," and "encens," whatever differences or gradations one wishes to establish between them, are refrained by "comme" ever to lead beyond themselves; the enumeration could be continued at will without ceasing to be a repetition, without ceasing to be an obsession rather than a metamorphosis, let alone a rebirth. One wonders if the evil connotations of these corrupt scents do not stem from the syntax rather than from the Turkish bath or black mass atmosphere one would otherwise have to conjure up. For what could be more perverse or corruptive for a metaphor aspiring to transcendental totality than remaining stuck in an enumeration that never goes anywhere? If number can only be conquered by another number, if identity becomes enumeration, then there is no conquest at all, since the stated purpose of the passage to infinity was, as in Pascal, to restore the one, to escape the tyranny of number by dint of infinite multiplication. Enumerative repetition disrupts the chain of tropological substitution at the crucial moment when the poem promises, by way of these very substitutions, to reconcile the pleasures of the mind with those of the senses and to unite aesthetics with epistemology. That the very word on which these substitutions depend would just then lose its syntactical and semantic univocity is too striking a coincidence not to be, like pure chance, beyond the control of author and reader.

It allows, at any rate, for a sobering literalization of the word "transport" in the final line "Qui chantent les transports de l'esprit et des sens." "Transport" here means, of course, to be carried away beyond thought and sensation in a common transcendental realm; it evokes loss of control and ecstatic unreason. But all attentive readers of Baudelaire have always felt that this claim at self-loss is not easily compatible with a colder, analytic self-consciousness that moves in a very different direction. In the words of our text, "les transports de l'esprit" and "Les transports des sens" are not at all the same "transports." We have learned to recognize, of late, in "transports" the spatial displacement implied by the verbal ending of meta-*phorein*. One is reminded that, in the French-speaking cities of our century, "correspondance" meant, on the trolley-cars, the equivalence of what is called in English a "transfer"—the privilege, automatically granted on the Paris Métro, of connecting from one line to another without having to buy a new ticket.

The prosaic transposition of ecstasy to the economic codes of public transportation is entirely in the spirit of Baudelaire and not by itself disruptive with regard to the claim for transcendental unity. For the transfer indeed merges two different displacements into one single system of motion and circulation, with corresponding economic and metaphysical profits. The problem is not so much centered on *phorein* as on *meta* (trans . . .), for does "beyond" here mean a movement beyond some particular place or does it mean a state that is beyond movement entirely? And how can "beyond," which posits and names movement, ever take us away from what it posits? The question haunts the text in all its ambiguities, be it "passer à travers" or the discrepancy between the "comme" of homogeneity and the "comme" of enumeration. The apparent rest and tranquility of "Correspondances" within the corpus of *Les Fleurs du Mal* lies indeed beyond tension and beyond motion. If Nature is truly a temple, it is not a means of transportation or a railroad station, Victorian architects who loved to build railroad stations in the shape of cathedrals notwithstanding. Nature in this poem is not a road toward a temple, a sequence of motions that take up there. Its travels, whatever they are, lie far behind us; there is no striving here, no questing for an absence or a presence. And if man (l'homme) is at home among "regards familiers" within that Nature, then his language of tropes and analogies is of little use to them. In this realm, transfer tickets are of no avail. Within the confines of a system of transportation—or of language as a system of communication—one can transfer from one vehicle to another, but one cannot transfer from being like a vehicle to being like a temple, or a ground.

The epistemological, aesthetic, and poetic language of transports or of tropes, which is the theme though not singly the rhetoric of this poem, can never say nor, for that matter, sing or understand the opening statement: "la Nature est un temple." But the poem offers no explicit alternative to this language which, like the perfumes enumerated by "comme," remains condemned to the repetition of its superfluity. Few poems in *Les Fleurs du Mal* state this in a manner that is both so obvious yet, by necessity, so oblique. The poem most remote from stating it is also the one closest to "Correspondances," its "echo" as it were, with which it is indeed very easy to confuse it. Little clarity can be gained from "Correspondances" except for the knowledge that disavows its deeper affinity with "Obsession."

Written presumably in February 1860, at least five years after "Correspondances" (of which the date is uncertain but anterior to 1855), "Obsession" alludes to many poems in *Les Fleurs du Mal*, such as "l'Homme et la mer" (1852) and "De profundis clamavi" (1851). But it more than alludes to "Correspondances"; it can be called a *reading* of the earlier text, with all the complications that are inherent in this term. The relationship between the two poems can indeed be seen as the construction and the undoing of the mirrorlike, specular structure that is always involved in a reading. On both the thematic and the rhetorical level, the reverted symmetries between the two texts establish their correspondence along a positive/negative axis. Here again, our problem is centered on the possibility of reinscribing into the system elements, in either text, that do not belong to this pattern. The same question can be asked in historical or in generic terms but, in so doing, the significance of this terminology risks being unsettled.

One can, for instance, state the obvious difference in theme and in diction between the two poems in terms derived from the canonical history of French nineteenth-century lyric poetry. With its portal of Greek columns, its carefully balanced symmetries, and its decorous absence of any displayed emotion, "Correspondances" has all the characteristics of a Parnassian poem, closer to Heredia than to Hugo. The "romantic" exaltation of "Obsession" 's apostrophes and exclamations, on the other hand, is self-evident. If nature is a "transport" in "Obsession," it is a temple in "Correspondances." However, by putting the two texts side by side in this manner, their complementarity is equally manifest. What is lost in personal expressiveness from the first poem is gained in the symbolic "depth" that has prompted comparisons of "Correspondances" with the poetry of that other neo-classicist, Gérard de Nerval, or supported the claim of its being the forerunner of symbolism. Such a historicizing pattern, a commonplace of aesthetic theory, is a function of the aesthetic ideologization of linguistic structures rather than an empirical historical event. The dialectical interaction of "classical" with "romantic" conceptions, as summarized in the contrastive symmetries between these two sonnets, ultimately reveals the symbolic character of poetic language, the linguistic structure in which it is rooted. "Symbolist" art is considered archaic when it is supposed to be spontaneous, modern when it is self-conscious, and this terminology has a certain crude wisdom about it that is anything but historical, however, in its content. Such a combination of linguistic with pseudo-historical terms, of "symbolic" with "classic" (or *parnassien*) or with "romantic" (or *symboliste*), a combination familiar at least since Hegel's *Lectures on Aesthetics*, is a necessary feature of systems that combine tropes with aesthetic and epistemological norms. In this perspective, the relationship between the neo-classical "Correspondances" and the post-romantic "Obsession" is itself structured like a symbol: the two sonnets complement each other like the two halves of a *symbolon*. Historicizing them into a diachrony or into a valorized qualitative hierarchy is more convenient than it is legitimate. The terminology of traditional literary history, as a succession of periods or literary movements, remains useful only if the terms are seen for what they are: rather crude metaphors for figural patterns rather than historical events or acts.

Stated in generic rather than historical terms, the relationship between "Correspondances" and "Obsession" touches upon the uncertain status of the lyric as a term for poetic discourse in general. The lyric's claim of being song is made explicitly in "Correspondances" ("qui *chantent* les transports . . ."), whereas "Obsession" howls, laughs, and speaks but does not pretend to sing. Yet the *je-tu* structure of the syntax makes it much closer to the representation of a vocal utterance than the engraved, marmorean gnomic wisdom of "Correspondances." The reading however disclosed a discrepancy that affects the verb "chanter" in the concluding line: the suggestive identification of "parfum" with song, based on common resonance and expansion, is possible only within a system of relays and transfers that, in the syntax if not in the stated meaning of the poem, becomes threatened by the stutter, the *piétinement* of aimless enumeration. This eventuality, inherent in the structure of the tropes on which the claim to lyricism depends, conflicts with the monumental stability of a completed entity that exists independently of its principle of constitution and destruction. Song is not compatible with aphasia and a stuttering Amphion is an absurd figure indeed. No lyric can be read lyrically nor can the object of a lyrical reading be itself a lyric— which implies least of all that it is epical or dramatic. Baudelaire's own lyrical reading of "Correspondances," however, produced at least a text, the sonnet entitled "Obsession."

The opening of "Obsessions" reads the first quatrain of "Correspondances" as if it were indeed a sylvan scene. It naturalizes the surreal speech of live columns into the frightening, but natural, roar of the wind among the trees:

> Grands bois, vous m'effrayez comme des cathédrales;
> Vous hurlez comme l'orgue;

The benefits of naturalization—as we can call the reversal of anthropomorphism—are at once apparent. None of the uncertainties that obscure the opening lines of "Correspondances" are maintained. No "comme" could be more orthodox than the two "commes" in these two lines. The analogism is so perfect that the implied anthropomorphism becomes fully motivated.

In this case, the unifying element is the wind as it is heard in whistling keyholes, roaring trees, and wind instruments such as church organs. Neither is there any need to invoke hallucination to account for the fear inspired by stormy forests and huge cathedrals: both are versions of the same dizziness of vast spaces. The adjustment of the elements involved (wood, wind, fear, cathedral, and organ) is perfectly self-enclosed, since all the pieces in the structure fit each other: wood and cathedral share a common shape, but wood also fits organ by way of the noise of the roaring wind; organ and cathedral, moreover, are linked by metonymy, etc. Everything can be substituted for everything else without distorting the most natural experience. Except, of course, for the "vous" of address in the apostrophe "Grands bois," which is, of course, absurd from a representational point of view; we are all frightened by windy woods but do not generally make a spectacle of ourselves talking to trees.

Yet the power of the analogy, much more immediately compelling than that of synesthesia in "Correspondances," naturalizes even this most conventional trope of lyric address: when it is said, in line 4, that the terror of the wind corresponds to the subjective fear of death

> et dans nos coeurs maudits,
>
> . . .
>
> Répondent les échos de vos *De profundis*,

then the analogy between outer event and inner feeling is again so close that the figural distance between noise (wind) and speech or even music almost vanishes, all the more so since wind as well as death are designated by associated sounds: the howling of the wind and the penitential prayer, aural metonymy for death. As a result, the final attribution of speech to the woods (*vos* De profundis) appears so natural that it takes an effort to notice that anthropomorphism is involved. The claim to verbality in the equivalent line from "Correspondances," "Les parfums, les couleurs et les sons se répondent" seems fantastic by comparison. The omnipresent metaphor of interiorization, of which this is a striking example, here travels initially by ways of the ear alone.

The gain in pathos is such as to make the depth of *De profundis* the explicit theme of the poem. Instead of being the infinite expanse, the openness of "Vaste comme la nuit et comme la clarté," depth is now the enclosed space that, like the sound chamber of a violin, produces the inner vibration of emotion. We retrieve what was conspicuously absent from "Correspondances," the recurrent image of the subject's presence to itself as a spatial enclosure, room, tomb, or crypt in which the voice echoes as in a cave. The image draws its verisimilitude from its own "mise en abîme" in the shape of the body as the *container* of the voice (or soul, heart, breath, consciousness, spirit, etc.) that it exhales. At the cost of much represented agony ("Chambres d'éternel deuil où vibrent de vieux râles"), "Obsession" asserts its right to say "I" with full authority. The canon of Romantic and post-Romantic lyric poetry offers innumerable versions and variations of this inside/outside pattern of exchange that founds the metaphor of the lyrical voice as subject. In a parallel movement, reading interiorizes the meaning of the text by its understanding. The union of aesthetic with epistemological properties is carried out by the mediation of the metaphor of the self as consciousness of itself, which implies its negation.

The specular symmetry of the two texts is such that any instance one wishes to select at once involves the entire system with flawless consistency. The hellenic "temple" of "Correspondances," for example, becomes the Christian "cathédrale" of "Obsession," just as the denominative, impersonal third person discourse of the earlier poem becomes the first person discourse of the later one. The law of this figural and chiastic transformation is negation. "Obsession" self-consciously denies and rejects the sensory wealth of "Correspondances." The landscape of denial from "De profundis clamavi":

> C'est un pays plus nu que la terre polaire;
> —Ni bêtes, ni ruisseaux, ni verdure, ni bois!

reappears as the desire of "Obsession":

> Car je cherche le vide, et le noir, et le nu!

in sharp denial of

> Doux comme les hautbois, verts comme les prairies

from "Correspondances." Similar negations pervade the texts, be it in terms of affects, moods, or grammar.

The negation, however, is indeed a figure of chiasmus, for the positive and negative valorizations can be distributed on both sides. We read "Obsession" thematically as an interiorization of "Correspondances," and as a negation of the positivity of an outside reality. But it is just as plausible to consider "Obsession" as the making manifest, as the exteriorization of the subject that remains hidden in "Correspondances." Naturalization, which appears to be a movement from inside to outside, allows for affective verisimilitude which moves in the opposite direction. In terms of figuration also, it can be said that "Correspondances" is the negation of "Obsession": the figural stability of "Obsession" is denied in "Correspondances." Such patterns constantly recur in nineteenth- and twentieth-century lyric poetry and create a great deal of critical confusion, symptomatic of further-reaching complexities.

The recuperative power of the subject metaphor in "Obsession" becomes particularly evident, in all its implications, in the tercets. As soon as the sounds of words are allowed, as in the opening stanza, to enter into analogical combinations with the sounds of nature, they necessarily turn into the light imagery of representation and of knowledge. If the sounds of nature are akin to those of speech, then nature also speaks by ways of light, the light of the senses as well as of the mind. The philosophical phantasm that has concerned us throughout this reading, the reconciliation of knowledge with phenomenal, aesthetic experience, is summarized in the figure of speaking light which, as is to be expected in the dialectical mode of negation, is both denied and asserted:

> Comme tu me plairais, ô nuit! sans ces étoiles
> Dont *la lumière parle* un langage connu!

Light implies space which, in turn, implies the possibility of spatial differentiation, the play of distance and proximity that organizes perception as the foreground-background juxtaposition that links it to the aesthetics of painting. Whether the light emanates from outside us before it is interiorized by the eye, as is the case here in the perception of a star, or whether the light emanates from inside and projects the entity, as in hallucination or in certain dreams, makes little difference in this context. The metamorphic crossing between perception and hallucination

> Mais les ténèbres sont elles-mêmes des toiles
> Où vivent, jaillissant de mon oeil par milliers,
> Des êtres disparus aux regards familiers

occurs by means of the paraphernalia of painting, which is also that of recollection and of re-cognition, as the recovery, to the senses, of what seemed to be forever beyond experience. In an earlier outline, Baudelaire had written

> Mais les ténèbres sont elles-mêmes des toiles
> Où [peint] . . . (presumably for "se peignent")

"Peint" confirms the reading of "toiles" as the device by means of which
painters or dramatists project the space or the stage of representation, by
enframing the interiorized expanse of the skies. The possibility of representation asserts itself at its most efficacious at the moment when the sensory
plenitude of "Correspondances" is most forcefully denied. The lyric depends
entirely for its existence on the denial of phenomenality as the surest means
to recover what it denies. This motion is not dependent, in its failure or in
its illusion of success, on the good or the bad faith of the subject it constitutes.

The same intelligibility enlightens the text when the enigma of consciousness as eternal mourning ("Chambres d'éternel deuil où vibrent de
vieux râles") is understood as the hallucinatory obsession of recollection,
certainly easier to comprehend by shared experience than by esoteric *correspondances*. "Obsession" translates "Correspondances" into intelligibility,
the least one can hope for in a successful reading. The resulting couple or
pair of texts indeed becomes a model for the uneasy combination of funereal
monumentality with paranoid fear that characterizes the hermeneutics and
the pedagogy of lyric poetry.

Yet, this very title, "Obsession," also suggests a movement that may
threaten the far-reaching symmetry between the two texts. For the temporal
pattern of obsessive thought is directly reminiscent of the tautological, enumerative stutter we encountered in the double semantic function of "comme,"
which disrupted the totalizing claim of metaphor in "Correspondances." It
suggests a psychological and therefore intelligible equivalent of what there
appeared as a purely grammatical distinction, for there is no compelling
thematic suggestion, in "comme l'ambre, le musc, le benjoin et l'encens,"
that allows one to think of this list as compulsively haunting. The title
"Obsession," or the last line of the poem, which names the ghostly memory
of mourned absences, does therefore not correspond to the tension, deemed
essential, between the expansiveness of "des choses infinies" and the restrictive catalogue of certain kinds of scents introduced by "comme." Yet, if the
symmetry between the two texts is to be truly recuperative, it is essential
that the disarticulation that threatens the first text should find its counterpart
in the second: mere naturalization of a grammatical structure, which is how
the relationship between enumeration and obsession can be understood, will
not suffice, since it is precisely the tension between an experienced and a
purely linguistic disruption that is at issue. There ought to be a place, in
"Obsession," where a similar contrast between infinite totalization and end-

less repetition of the same could be pointed out. No such place exists. At the precise point where one would expect it, at the moment when obsession is stressed in terms of number, "Obsession" resorts to synthesis by losing itself in the vagueness of the infinite

> Où vivent, jaillissant de mon oeil *par milliers*,
> Des êtres disparus aux regards familiers.

There could be no more decisive contrast, in *Les Fleurs du Mal*, than between the reassuring indeterminacy of these infinite thousands—as one had, in "Correspondances," "des forêts"—and the numerical precision with which, in "Les sept vieillards," it is the passage from one altogether finite to another altogether finite number that produces genuine terror:

> Aurais-je, sans mourir, contemplé le huitième,
> Sosie inexorable, ironique et fatal,
> Dégoûtant Phénix, fils et père de lui-même?
> —Mais je tournai le dos au cortège infernal.
>
> Exaspéré comme un ivrogne qui voit double,
> Je rentrai, je fermai ma porte, épouvanté,
> Malade et morfondu, l'esprit fiévreux et trouble,
> Blessé par le mystère et par l'absurdité!

Unlike "Obsession," "Les sept vieillards" can however in no respect be called a reading of "Correspondances," to which it in no way corresponds.

The conclusion is written into the argument which is itself written into the reading, a process of translation or "transport" that incessantly circulates between the two texts. There always are at least two texts, regardless of whether they are actually written out or not; the relationship between the two sonnets, obligingly provided by Baudelaire for the benefit, no doubt, of future teachers invited to speak on the nature of the lyric, is an inherent characteristic of any text. Any text, as text, compels reading as its understanding. What we call the lyric, the instance of represented voice, conveniently spells out the rhetorical and thematic characteristics that make it the paradigm of a complementary relationship between grammar, trope, and theme. The set of characteristics includes the various structures and moments we encountered along the way: specular symmetry along an axis of assertion and negation (to which correspond the generic mirror-images of the ode, as celebration, and the elegy, as mourning), the grammatical transformation of the declarative into the vocative modes of question, exclamation, address, hypothesis, etc., the tropological transformation of analogy into apostrophe or the equivalent, more general transformation which, with Nietzsche's assistance, we took as our point of departure: the transformation of trope into anthropomorphism. The lyric is not a genre, but one name among several to designate the defensive motion of understanding, the possibility of a future hermeneutics. From this point of view, there is no significant difference between one generic term and another: all have the same apparently intentional and temporal function.

We all perfectly and quickly understand "Obsession," and better still the motion that takes us from the earlier to the later text. But no symmetrical reversal of this lyrical reading-motion is conceivable; if Baudelaire, as is eminently possible, were to have written, in empirical time, "Correspondances" after "Obsession," this would change nothing. "Obsession" derives from "Correspondances" but the reverse is not the case. Neither does it account for it as its origin or cause. "Correspondances" implies and explains "Obsession" but "Obsession" leaves "Correspondances" as thoroughly incomprehensible as it always was. In the paraphernalia of literary terminology, there is no term available to tell us what "Correspondances" might be. All we know is that it is, emphatically, *not* a lyric. Yet it, and it alone, contains, implies, produces, generates, permits (or whatever aberrant verbal metaphor one wishes to choose) the entire possibility of the lyric. Whenever we encounter a text such as "Obsession"—that is, whenever we read—there always is an infra-text, a hypogram like "Correspondances" underneath. Stating this relationship, as we just did, in phenomenal, spatial terms or in phenomenal, temporal terms—"Obsession," a text of recollection and elegiac mourning, *adds* remembrance to the flat surface of time in "Correspondances"—produces at once a hermeneutic, fallacious lyrical reading of the unintelligible. The power that takes one from one text to the other is not just a power of displacement, be it understood as recollection or interiorization or any other "transport," but the sheer blind violence that Nietzsche, concerned with the same enigma, domesticated by calling it, metaphorically, an *army* of tropes.

Generic terms such as "lyric" (or its various sub-species, "ode," "idyll," or "elegy") as well as pseudo-historical period terms such as "romanticism" or "classicism" are always terms of resistance and nostalgia, at the furthest remove from the materiality of actual history. If mourning is called a "chambre d'éternel deuil où vibrent de vieux râles," then this pathos of terror states in fact the desired consciousness of eternity and of temporal harmony as voice and as song. True "mourning" is less deluded. The most *it* can do is to allow for non-comprehension and enumerate non-anthropomorphic, non-elegiac, non-celebratory, non-lyrical, non-poetic, that is to say, prosaic, or, better, *historical* modes of language power.

HELEN REGUEIRO ELAM

Temporality in Baudelaire

> denn Blumen giebt es,
> Nicht von der Erde gezeugt, von selber
> Aus lokerem Boden sprossen die,
> Ein Widerstral des Tages, nicht ist
> Es ziemend, diese zu pflüken
> Denn golden stehn schon
> Unzubereitet, die unbelaubten
> Gedanken gleich . . .

> (for there are flowers
> Not sprung from earth, from themselves
> Out of the empty soil they spring,
> A reflection of day, it is not
> Proper to pluck these
> For they stand golden
> Unprepared, disincarnated
> Like thoughts . . .)
> —HÖLDERLIN, *Tinian*

> The greatest poverty is not to live
> In a physical world, to feel that one's desire
> Is too difficult to tell from despair.
> —STEVENS, *Esthétique du Mal*

Temporality is an abiding concern in Baudelaire's poetry, and appears directly related to his conception of *Les Fleurs du Mal*. Criticism of these poems has focused persistently on the various possible referents for this title—the moral, the aesthetic, and so on—but has eschewed the more am-

© 1987 by Helen Regueiro Elam. Published for the first time in this volume.

143

biguous question of temporality itself. At first glance it appears that these
flowers of evil are products of temporality's effect on our lives. Time weakens
powerful emotions like pain and turns them into despair or "ennui." Yet
even as he laments the effects of temporality, Baudelaire privileges in *Les
Fleurs du Mal* those very objects which derive their power from the transformation and disintegration time has wrought upon them. In other word,
Baudelaire puts aside the romantic tendency to privilege the natural object
or the immediate experience, and privileges instead those objects, mediated
by time, which have no authenticity other than the transformation they have
undergone. In the Stevensian sense desire *is* too difficult to tell from despair
in Baudelaire's poetry, for desire and despair duplicate each other through
Les Fleurs du Mal.

> Et qui sait si les fleurs nouvelles que je rêve
> Trouveront dans ce sol lavé comme une grève
> Le mystique aliment qui ferait leur vigeur?
>
> —O douleur! ô douleur! Le Temps mange la vie,
> Et l'obscur Ennemi qui nous ronge le coeur
> Du sang que nous perdons croît et se fortifie!
>
> And who knows if the new flowers I dream of
> Will find in this washed out soil some strand line
> The mystic nourishment that would create their strength?
>
> —Oh sorrow! oh sorrow! Time eats away life,
> And the obscure enemy that gnaws at our heart
> Grows and is strengthened by the blood we lose!
>
> ("L'Ennemi")

These new flowers draw their strength from the empty soil of consciousness
and appear to constitute a triumph over time. Such a reading would tend to
separate these last two stanzas of the poem, with the last stanza functioning
as a negative response to the question of the preceding stanza. Yet the pin
and the obscure enemy (ennui) that gnaws at life is precisely the mystical
nourishment of these flowers. Time is not so much the enemy as the creator
of these flowers, objects, poems whose power (nourishment) is drawn from
the disruptive effect of time itself. The last stanza follows upon the preceding
one, and the apostrophe suggests that sorrow *is* that mystic nourishment the
poet seeks.

    This reversal of expectation operates across the *Fleurs du Mal*. Baudelaire appears to mourn an immediacy lost to the temporal perspective, and several major poems in the volume focus on objects transformed by time into something "other" than what they were, thus by their very "presence" bespeaking the absence of their being. Yet what is peculiar about this perspective of loss is that poems addressing such objects seem to invent a past whose loss the poet can then lament. Evocation of such a past takes priority over whatever that past may have been. In "La Chevelure," for instance, Baudelaire moves, in a series of metonymical leaps punctuated by exclamation marks, from the evocation of a woman's hair to an invocation of the power of "souvenir" itself to create a world that never existed in the past. Memory in Baudelaire is repeatedly transformed into prolepsis, and this transformation is achieved by what may be Baudelaire's favorite strategy: the apostrophe. An apostrophe invokes, addresses, assumes at once presence and absence, and eludes the normal syntax of the sentence.

> O toison, moutonnant jusque sur l'encolure!
> O boucles! O parfum chargé de nonchaloir!
> Extase! Pour peupler ce soir l'alcôve obscure
> Des souvenirs dormat dans cette chevelure
> Je la veux agiter dans l'air comme un mouchoir!
>
> (Oh fleece curling down to the neck!
> Oh curls! Oh perfume laden with heedlessness!
> Ecstasy! To people this evening the dark alcove
> With souvenirs sleeping in this head of hair,
> I want to shake it like a handkerchief in the air!)

Four apostrophes puncture the movement from "fleece" to curls to perfume to the poet's ecstasy, and are followed by a further leap to "souvenirs" and then to a handkerchief one waves in the wind, with the paradoxical farewell such gesture implies. The transport implicit in the figurative leaps and in the apostrophes seems to stem in this poem from a particular remembrance that is lost beyond telling. Yet Baudelaire remembers a particular "souvenir" in order to invent what has no presence—a dream world that has to be imagined as absence: "N'es tu-pas l'oasis où je rêve, et la gourde / Où je hume à longs traits le vin du souvenir?" ("Are you not the oasis I dream of, and the gourd / Where I inhale deeply from the wine of remembrance?") Remembrance is paradoxically prolepsis in Baudelaire, and in that sense it is a triumph over the temporal duration whose pressure he laments. Remembrance is figuration, and its gesture of farewell is at once its gesture of renewal.

More explicitly in "Le Balcon," the poet evokes a past which is constructed in the act of evocation. The poem makes insistent use of apostrophe, and each apostrophe appears to be lament and farewell.

> Mère des souvenirs, maîtresse des maîtresses,
> O toi, tous mes plaisirs! ô toi, tous mes devoirs!
> Tu te rappelleras la beauté des caresses,
> La douceur du foyer et le charme des soirs,
> Mère des souvenirs, maîtresse des maîtresses!
>
> . . . .
>
> Je sais l'art d'évoquer les minutes heureuses,
> Et revis mon passé blotti dans tes genoux.
> Car à quoi bon chercher tes beautés langoureuses
> Ailleurs qu'en ton cher corps et qu'en ton coeur si doux?
> Je sais l'art d'évoquer les minutes heureuses!
>
> Ces serments, ces parfums, ces baisers infinis,
> Renaîtront-ils d'un gouffre interdit à nos sondes,
> Comme montent au ciel les soleils rajeunis
> Après s'être lavés au fond des mers profondes?
> —O serments! ô parfums! ô baisers infinis!
>
> (Mother of memories, mistress of mistresses,
> Oh thou, all my pleasures! oh thou, all my duties!
> You will remember the beauty of caresses,
> The sweetness of hearth and the charm of evenings,
> Mother of memories, mistress of mistresses!
>
> . . . .
>
> I know the art of evoking happy moments,
> And relive my past doubled up by your knees.
> For what use to seek languid beauties
> Other than in your dear body and in your tender heart?
> I know the art of evoking happy moments!
>
> These oaths, these perfumes, these infinite kisses,
> Will they be reborn from an abyss barred to our soundings,
> As renewed suns climb the sky
> After washing themselves in the depth of deep seas?
> —Oh paths, oh perfumes! oh infinite kisses!)

Lament makes time appear a category of loss, and creates a picture of a barren present, bereft of the immediacy proclaimed by remembrance. The poet "resees" his past in the "presence" of the body of the beloved. But this re-seeing and re-presenting, appearing as they do to bring forth the past, are instead brought forth by the poet's "evocation." The word "evoke" is rich in French, suggesting both the remembrance of the past and the invocation (apostrophizing) of what lies at the origin of remembrance ("Mère des souvenirs"). Here the invocation/evocation is not of memory-as-mother but of the mother of memory, and the source of these "souvenirs" the poet evokes is itself contained within the act of evocation. The poem appears to come to rest on a series of memories ("Tu te rappelleras . . .") and indeed it opens with an invocation to the mother of remembrance. But the act of evocation widens and captures all memories within itself, so that it appears as the origin it attempts to invoke.

This containment is rendered stylistically by the repetition of the first and last lines in each stanza, and by the repeated use of apostrophe throughout the poem. The last line repeating the first closes the space of each stanza, and underscores the containment of "souvenir" within the act that supposedly represents or evokes it. To evoke for Baudelaire is to create an origin, to create a cause by referring to it as effect, and this reversal accounts for the syntactic breakdown several times in the poem: we expect a complete sentence, or at least a verb and complement, but the apostrophe breaks that expectation and breaks the syntax of the poem. Propelled by a noun and occasionally an adjective, the apostrophe eschews by and large the kind of syntax that would refer us back to past and present, cause and effect. Instead of invoking memory as the traditional mother of the muses, Baudelaire invokes the mother of memory and terms her his muse. Baudelaire seeks out the origin of memory as his muse, and evades the temporal perspective of cause and effect by propelling the poem through a series of disjunctive apostrophes. These apostrophes tell the story of a cause and effect reversal, for at the origin of memory Baudelaire finds not a memory but a moment of evocation—the very apostrophe by which the mother of memory is invoked. "Le Balcon" (in its double meaning of balcony and theater) thus posits itself as a self-originating poem. Indeed, "blotti" (doubled-up) may be the most telling image in the poem, in its suggestion of a self-reflexive being whose origins lie in its theatrical gestures.

This question of self-reflexivity haunts the poems of *Les Fleurs du Mal*, and becomes the question of poetry itself. In *Un Fantôme* the poet is painter and eater, painting "sur les ténèbres" and eating, with "funereal appetite," his own heart. The poet/painter feeds on his own interiority, his own "dark depths." Transitive verbs seem to disappear here, as all experience is referred back to a self feeding upon its phantomlike existence. In the second part of the poem, the trope of eating is extended into that of breathing, so that the perfume the poet breathes is digested by the body:

> Lecteur, as-tu quelquefois respiré
> Avec ivresse et lente gourmandise
> Ce grain d'encens qui remplit une église,
> Ou d'un sachet le musc invétéré?

> Charme profond, magique, dont nous grise
> Dans le présent le passé restauré!
> Ainsi l'amant sur un corps adoré
> Du souvenir cueille la fleur exquise.

> (Reader, have you some time breathed
> With drunkenness and slow gluttony
> This grain of incense which fills a church,
> Or the inveterate musk from a sachet?

> Profound charm, magical, with which
> The past restored to the present intoxicates us!
> Thus the lover on a beloved body
> Gathers the exquisite flower of remembrance.)

Perfume is itself a trope for the past "restored" into the present, but the trope refers to a peculiar restoration in which the lover gathers not sexual fulfillment from an erotic encounter but "the exquisite flower of remembrance." "Souvenir" is thus for Baudelaire not the result of an erotic encounter but its very cause. Freud suggests that we seek through our lives a love object we have imagined in the first place. The priority of the imagined is suggested in this poem by the priority of the remembrance or souvenir over any experience it might be said to represent. The past is thus not so much "restored" in Baudelaire as it is *imagined as past* under the guise of souvenir. Recollection, as in "Le Balcon," is the result of evocation. (The lover may well be encountering the body of remembrance *as* the beloved's body.) Remembrance in Baudelaire is given the ontological status of an object not only in the metonymical connections between remembrance/mind/body in this stanza but in the portrayal of remembrance *as* perfume, bottle, etc.— objects which assail the body's senses and draw the poet into the fiction of remembering and confronting what he has created: "Rien, hors moi, ne répond." ("Nothing, outside myself, responds.")

While perfume and perfume bottles appear in *Les Fleurs du Mal* as a centralizing, thematic concern, in each case the perfume or perfume bottle offers itself as the cause it purports to represent or stand for, so that behind or beneath these perfumes and bottles there is an absence which Baudelaire terms "death." "Le Flacon" puts this process of unveiling into evidence by focusing on the strategy of "souvenir."

> Il est de forts parfums pour qui toute matière
> Est poreuse. On dirait qu'ils pénètrent le verre.
> En ouvrant un coffret venu de l'Orient
> Dont la serrure grince et rechigne en criant,
>
> Ou dans une maison déserte quelque armoire
> Pleine de l'âcre odeur du temps, poudreuse et noire,
> Parfois on trouve un vieux flacon qui se souvient,
> D'où jaillit toute vive une âme qui revient.
>
> . . . .
>
> Voilà le souvenir enivrant qui voltige
> Dans l'air troublé; les yeux se ferment; le Vertige
> Saisit l'âme vaincue et la pousse à deux mains
> Vers un gouffre obscurci de miasmes humains.
>
> . . . .
>
> Je serai ton cercueil, aimable pestilence!
> Le témoin de ta force et de ta virulence,
> Cher poison préparé par les anges! liqueur
> Qui me ronge, ô la vie et la mort de mon coeur!
>
> (There are strong perfumes for which all matter
> Is porous. One would say they penetrate glass.
> Opening a chest come from the Orient
> Whose lock grates and sullenly resists,
>
> Or in a deserted house some closet
> Full of the acrid smell of time, dusty and black,
> Sometimes one finds an old bottle that remembers,
> From which breaks forth alive a soul that returns.
>
> . . . .
>
> There is the inebriating memory which flutters
> In the troubled air; eyes close; Vertigo
> Takes hold of the vanquished soul and pushes it
> Towards an abyss darkened by human emanations.
>
> . . . .

I will be your tomb, friendly pestilence!
Witness to your power and your virulence,
Dear poison prepared by angels! liquor
That eats at me, oh life and death of my heart!)

Souvenir is in French a particular remembrance or act of memory, but it
has taken on for us both in English and in French the notion of an object.
We speak of bringing home a souvenir from some alien place that we have
visited, as if the object held for us in compressed form the collection of
experiences in another place. We assume, of course, that first comes the
experience, and then the souvenir, as a representation (photo), summary, or
metonymical relation to the place. But what happens when the souvenir
becomes more powerful than any experience, as Susan Stewart suggests,
when of itself it acquires priority over anything it might represent? The
souvenir for Baudelaire becomes an object that has no authenticity other
than the transformation and the disintegration brought upon it by time.
Indeed, it is this presumed "loss" that constitutes its authenticity and gives
it its power. Where romantic poets tended to privilege and to seek out
unmediated experience, Baudelaire has a predilection for objects that bespeak
a disintegration of direct experience, such that experience can be said to be
radically mediated by time. Thus the power of perfume/souvenir in this
poem lies not in its link to the past, but in the power of disintegration itself,
which makes the souvenir as present object stronger than the reality from
which it was extracted. "Pestilence" is drawn from perfume, yet it obliterates
its origin and overpowers the present.

   In turn this creates an ambiguous relation between souvenir as object
and souvenir as memory. The perfume's presence as pestilence (what it has
become) constitutes the perfume's absence as perfume. The souvenir epito-
mizes the absence of the object it purportedly represents. More importantly,
this overpowering extends from the perfume/bottle relationship to that between poetry and the poem. When the poem begins "Il est de forts parfums
pour qui toute matière / Est poreuse," the referent is of course the perfume
bottle, but also the poem as text, whose porous quality, in opposition to any
thematic, centralizing concerns, permits poetry to escape the confines of the
poem. Baudelaire's forms and rhymes are rather traditional, but his tropes
are less so. The poet in this poem is finally the vessel for this perfume/
pestilence whose transport in time will attest to the power of poetry. For all
its rhyme and meter, the porous matter of the text will yield to the power
of poetry, and to the power of critical reading to reinvent that lost and
imagined object ("hypocrite lecteur, mon semblable, mon frère"). The poem

begins with a meditation on the power of the object to "remember" the past, but to remember it in its own way, so that the past as such does not exist. It ends with a projection of the poem into the future which duplicates the opening movement from past to present. Poet, poem, bottle, coffin—the metaphorical relations are porous indeed, and that "difference" which does not permit identity makes possible, instead, the proleptic moment: the poet will become the container for that power/poison/poetry which assails and disintegrates him. He, too, will become porous matter, a re-presentation to the reader of the text called Baudelaire. The poetry/poison eats at him ("me ronge"), and the absence we call death and the presence we call life are folded here in a single party which is the text of the poem. The porous text is the vehicle for a re-presentation that has no origin outside the act of representation itself. And thus the soul "jaillit toute vive," bursts forth from the poem/bottle, for that is finally where the soul really is. Out of the empty soil of consciousness spring the flowers which Hölderlin terms "not proper to pluck." For Baudelaire, plucking them produces vertigo ("le Vertige/Saisit l'âme vaincue"), for to pluck them involves a contemplation of the abyss. Flowers of evil are flowers of consciousness for whom memory and representation create the objects to which they presumably refer, bringing them forth against the backdrop of the abyss.

This abyss (the priority of the act of memory over what is remembered) takes on the name in *Fleurs du Mal* alternately of death and ennui, though Baudelaire attempts to separate them and to make one the transcendence of the other. Ennui is conventionally translated as boredom, but in Baudelaire it is connected with a vague dread without cause—for the dread stems precisely from the condition of an absent cause. If evocation can take priority over a remembered experience, then this vague dread is not just an existential but an aesthetic phenomenon—the condition of metaphor itself. Freud's anxiety before cause ("Angst vor etwas") is the psychic equivalent of this condition. The subsumption of cause into effect leads to a series of confusions, the most important of which is that of the living and the dead. In "Spleen LXXVI" the poet describes himself as living matter surrounded by vague dread ("matière vivante . . . un granit entouré d'une vague épouvante"). Living matter which is also granite, dead matter: this "Spleen" poem posits a confusion of living and dead, past and present, cause and effect, which is the very condition of ennui. Hölderlin's flowers sprung from themselves are the appropriate expression of this vague dread that cannot be accounted for except in terms of itself, and whose persistence shuts out the possibility of newness, or even death. Ennui describes in Baudelaire the poetic act, at the same time that the poetic act seeks to break the condition that constitutes it.

Death in this scheme would be a radical break from ennui, yet Baudelaire
finds these opposites drawn into one another, into the same confusion op-
erating between cause and effect.

The last poem of *Les Fleurs du Mal* is "Le Voyage," and the last section
of the poem is an apostrophe to death as a radical newness that will break
the condition of ennui:

> O Mort, vieux capitaine, il est temps! levons l'ancre.
> Ce pays nous ennuie, ô Mort! Appareillons!
> Si le ciel et la mer sont noirs comme de l'encre,
> Nos coeurs que tu connais sont remplis de rayons!
>
> Verse-nous ton poison pour qu'ils nous reconforte!
> Nous voulons, tant ce feu nous brûle le cerveau,
> Plonger au fond du gouffre, Enfer ou Ciel, qu'importe?
> Au fond de l'Inconnu pour trouver du *nouveau!*
>
> (Oh death, old captain, it is time! let's weigh anchor.
> This land vexes us, oh death! Let's get under way!
> If the sky and the sea are black as ink,
> Our hearts, which you know, are full of light!
>
> Pour us your poison so we will be revived!
> We want, so long as [so much] this fire burns in our brain,
> To plunge to the depths of the abyss, Hell or Heaven, what
>   matter?
> To the depths of the Unknown to find the *new!*)

The true voyage for Baudelaire is one without aim, he says earlier in the
poem, because such a voyage suggests the fatality of voyage and mirrors the
literary condition itself. Indeed, the sky and sea are written in black ink,
and the final text of *Fleurs du Mal* recapitulates and begins the volume,
repeating the condition of its voyage. Travelers in this poem search for what
has not yet been given a name ("de vastes voluptés . . . dont l'esprit humain
n'a jamais su le nom"), for a radical innocence beyond the trope. That radical
innocence, this final section suggests, is to be found only in death. Here the
poet apostrophizes death and asks for its poison (its poetry) so that newness
may break. The condition of ennui is for Baudelaire the condition of metaphor, and at the end of *Les Fleurs du Mal* he asks poetry to yield to him the
"poison" of the most radical newness, in order to find "presence" in the
absence called death. Like Whitman's "death, death, death, death, death" as

the mother, like Stevens's "the poem, the mother's presence, fills the room," Baudelaire's apostrophe demands of poetry an absolute beyond the tropological movement which is the voyage—beyond the very power of evocation by which both souvenir and death are invoked. But just as poison is the distilled essence of perfume, so is death the distilled essence of ennui. Baudelaire finally demands a transcendence of metaphor, but he achieves his radical newness by an intensification of metaphor and a production of the flowers of ennui.

Chronology

1821	Charles-Pierre Baudelaire is born in Paris on April 9, to Joseph-François Baudelaire and Caroline Archimbaut-Defayis.
1827	Baudelaire's father dies.
1828	Baudelaire's mother marries Major Jacques Aupick.
1832–39	Goes to school, first in Lyons, then in Paris.
1839	Expelled from college on April 18.
1840–41	Enrolled at law school. He runs up debts and contracts syphilis.
1841	Baudelaire's mother and stepfather send him abroad to India.
1842	Returns to France, having cut short his trip at Reunion Island. He receives the fortune left him by his father but squanders most of it and settles on the Ile Saint-Louis. He frequents literary and artistic circles, and forms his liaison with Jeanne Duval.
1844	Baudelaire's finances are put in trust of Narcisse-Désiré Ancelle.
1845	Publishes his first art criticism, *Le Salon de 1845*, in April.
1846	Publishes *Le Salon de 1846* in May.
1847	Publishes *La Fanfarlo*. Meets Marie Daubrun.
1848	Becomes involved in the current revolutionary movements.
1851	*Du Vin et du hachish*.
1852	Publishes *Edgar Allan Poe, sa Vie et ses Ouvrages* in *Revue de Paris*, and writes the first of a series of anonymous letters to Mme Sabatier.

1855   Publishes eighteen poems under the title of *Les Fleurs du Mal* in *La Revue des Deux Mondes*.

1856   Publishes *Histoires extraordinaires*, the first volume of his translations of Poe.

1857   *Nouvelles Histoires extraordinaires. Les Fleurs du Mal* goes on sale, and on August 20 Baudelaire goes to court to defend his work against charges of obscenity. He pays a fine, and six of the poems are suppressed. Later in the year he publishes six more prose poems. Relations with Mme Sabatier end.

1858   Publishes the first part of *Les Paradis artificiels*.

1859   Composes "Le Voyage" and "Le Cygne."

1860   *Les Paradis artificiels.*

1861   The second edition of *Les Fleurs du Mal* appears.

1862   Swinburne publishes an enthusiastic essay on *Les Fleurs du Mal*.

1864   Moves to Brussels.

1866   Baudelaire has a stroke, suffers from aphasia, and enters a nursing home.

1867   Charles Baudelaire dies on August 31.

Contributors

HAROLD BLOOM, Sterling Professor of the Humanities at Yale University, is the author of *The Anxiety of Influence*, *Poetry and Repression*, and many other volumes of literary criticism. His forthcoming study, *Freud: Transference and Authority*, attempts a full-scale reading of all of Freud's major writings. A MacArthur Prize Fellow, he is general editor of five series of literary criticism published by Chelsea House.

GEORGES BATAILLE was a distinguished French novelist and literary critic. His novels include several works of surrealistic and erotic literature, including *My Mother* and *Story of the Eye*, while *Literature and Evil* is his best known critical work.

VICTOR BROMBERT is the author of *The Intellectual Hero* and the former Chairman of the Yale University French Department. He has written extensively on Stendhal and Flaubert.

BARBARA JOHNSON teaches in the French Department at Harvard University. She is the author of *Défigurations: du langage poétique* and the translator of Jacques Derrida's *La Dissemination*.

GEORGES POULET held doctorates in both law and letters from the University of Liège. He taught at the University of Edinburgh, Johns Hopkins University, and the Universities of Zurich and Nice.

ROSEMARY LLOYD teaches at Cambridge University.

BERNARD HOWELLS is a lecturer in the French Department at King's College, London.

MARY ANN CAWS is Professor of French at Hunter College and the Graduate Center of the City University of New York. Her books include *The Poetry of Dada and Surrealism* and *The Inner Theater of Recent French Poetry*.

PAUL DE MAN was Sterling Professor of Comparative Literature at Yale University. His many works of literary theory and criticism include *Blindness and Insight*, *Allegories of Reading*, and *The Rhetoric of Romanticism*.

HELEN REGUEIRO ELAM is Professor of English at the State University of New York, Albany.

Bibliography

Ahearn, Edward J. "Black Woman, White Poet: Exile and Exploitation in Baudelaire's Jeanne Duval Poems." *The French Review* 51 (1977): 212–20.

Auerbach, Erich. "The Aesthetic Dignity of the *Fleurs du Mal*." Translated by Ralph Manheim. In *Scenes from the Drama of European Literature*. Minneapolis: University of Minnesota Press, 1984.

Aynesworth, Donald. "Humanity and Monstrosity in *Le Spleen de Paris*: A Reading of Mademoiselle Bistouri." *Romanic Review* 73 (1982): 209–21.

Balakian, Anna. "Fragments on Reality by Baudelaire and Breton." *New York Literary Forum* 8–9 (1981): 101–9.

Bandy, W. T. "Whitman and Baudelaire." *Walt Whitman Quarterly Review* 1, no. 3 (December 1983): 53–56.

Bataille, Georges. "Baudelaire." In *Literature and Evil*. Translated by Alistair Hamilton. London: Calder & Boyers, 1973.

Baudelaire, Charles. *Art in Paris 1845–1862*. Translated by Jonathon Mayne. London: Phaidon Press, 1965.

Benjamin, Walter. *Charles Baudelaire: A Lyric Poet in the Era of High Capitalism*. Translated by Harry Zohn. London: New Left Books, 1973.

Bersani, Leo. *Baudelaire and Freud*. Berkeley: University of California Press, 1977.

Block, Haskell M. "Poe, Baudelaire, Mallarmé, and the Problem of the Untranslatable." In *Translation Perspectives: Selected Papers, 1982–1983*. Edited by Marilyn Gaddis Rose. Binghamton, N.Y.: Translation Research and Instruction Program, State University of New York at Binghamton, 1984.

Burton, Richard D. *The Context of Baudelaire's "Le Cygne."* Durham: University of Durham, 1980.

Butor, Michel. *Histoire extraordinaire: essai sur un rêve de Baudelaire*. Paris: Gallimard, 1961.

Chase, Cynthia. "Getting Versed: Reading Hegel with Baudelaire." *Studies in Romanticism* 22 (Summer 1983): 241–66.

————. "Paragon, Parergon: Baudelaire Translates Rousseau." *Diacritics* 11, no. 2 (Summer 1981): 42–51.

Chesters, Graham. "A Political Reading of Baudelaire's 'L'Artiste inconnu' ('Le Guignon')." *The Modern Language Review* 79 (January 1984): 64–76.

de Man, Paul. *Blindness and Insight: Essays in the Rhetoric of Contemporary Criticism*. Rev. 2d Ed. Minneapolis: University of Minnesota Press, 1983.

Eliot, T. S. "Baudelaire." In *Selected Essays*. New Ed. New York: Harcourt, Brace & World, 1964.

Emmanuel, Pierre. *Baudelaire: The Paradox of Redemptive Satanism*. Translated by Robert T. Cargo. University: The University of Alabama Press, 1970.

L'Esprit créateur 13, no. 2 (1973).

Fried, Michael. "Painting Memories: On the Containment of the Past in Baudelaire and Manet." *Critical Inquiry* 10 (March 1984): 510–42.

Galand, René. "Baudelaire and Myth." In *The Binding of Proteus: Perspectives on Myth and the Literary Process*. Edited by Marjorie W. McCure, Tucker Orbison, and Philip M. Withim. Lewisburg, Pa.: Bucknell University Press, 1980.

Gilman, Margaret. *Baudelaire the Critic*. New York: Columbia University Press, 1943.

Godfrey, Sima. "Foules Rush In . . . Lamartine, Baudelaire and the Crowd." *Romance Notes* 24 (Fall 1983): 33–42.

Heck, Francis S. "Baudelaire and Proust: Chance Encounters of the Same Kind." *Nottingham French Studies* 23, no. 2 (October 1984): 17–26.

———. "Baudelaire's 'Confiteor' and the Reader." *Kentucky Romance Quarterly* 31 (1984): 23–30.

Jakobson, Roman S. and Claude Levi-Strauss. "Charles Baudelaire's 'Les Chats.' " In *The Structuralists*. Edited by Richard and Fernande De George. New York: Doubleday & Co., 1972.

Jauss, Hans Robert. "The Poetic Text Within the Change of Horizons of Reading: The Example of Baudelaire's 'Spleen.' " In *Toward an Aesthetic of Reception*. Minneapolis: University of Minnesota Press, 1982.

Johnston, John H. *The Poet and the City: A Study in Urban Perspectives*. Athens: University of Georgia Press, 1984.

Kaplan, Edward K. "Baudelaire's Portrait of the Poet as Widow: Three Poèmes en Prose and 'Le Cygne.' " *Symposium* 34 (Fall 1980): 233–48.

King, Russell S. "De-Marginalizing a Throw-Away Line: Baudelaire's Heroic Soldier." *Nottingham French Studies* 23, no. 2 (October 1984): 9–16.

Klein, Richard. " 'Bénédiction'-'Perte d'Auréole': Parable of Interpretation." *MLN* 85 (May 1970): 515–28.

Knapp, Bettina. "Baudelaire and Delacroix: The Celebration of a Mystery." In *Writing in a Modern Temper: Essays on French Literature and Thought in Honor of Henri Peyre*. Edited by Mary Ann Caws. Saratoga, Calif.: Anma Libri, 1984.

Levitine, Eda Mezer. "Charles Baudelaire and Rodolphe Töpffer." *Swiss-French Studies* 4, no. 1 (May 1983): 31–41.

McKenna, Andrew. "Baudelaire and Nietzsche: Squaring the Circle of Madness." In *Pre-Text/Text/Context: Essays on Modern French Literature*. Edited by Robert L. Mitchell. Columbus: Ohio State University Press, 1980.

———. "Double Talk: Two Baudelairean Revolutions." *New Orleans Review* 10, no. 4 (Winter 1983): 99–108.

Murry, John Middleton. "Baudelaire." In *Countries of the Mind: Essays in Literary Criticism*. London: W. Collins Sons & Co. Ltd., 1922.

Odom, Billie Jean. "Perspectives in Translation: Baudelaire's Poem: 'La Cloche fêlée.' " *Translation Review* 15 (1984): 9–13.

Poulet, Georges. "Baudelaire." In *Exploding Poetry: Baudelaire-Rimbaud*. Translated by Françoise Meltzer. Chicago: University of Chicago Press, 1984.

Rao, N. M. "Baudelaire's Experiments With Time." *Journal of Comparative Literature and Aesthetics* 5, nos. 1–2 (1982): 87–94.

Reed, Arden. "Abysmal Influence: Baudelaire, Coleridge, De Quincey, Piranesi, Wordsworth." *Glyph* 4 (1978): 189–206.

———. "Baudelaire's 'La Pipe': De la vaporisation du *Moi*." *Romanic Review* 72 (1981): 274–84.

Richards, Sylvie. "The Conceits of Eyes and Hair in the French Decadence." *West Virginia University Philological Papers* 28 (1982): 41–48.

Riffaterre, Michael. "Describing Poetic Structures: Two Approaches to Baudelaire's 'Les Chats.' " In *Structuralism*. Edited by Jacques Ehrmann. Garden City, N.Y.: Doubleday, 1970.

Robb, Graham M. "Baudelaire and the Ghosts of Stone." *Romance Notes* 25 (Winter 1984): 137–44.

Sartre, Jean-Paul. *Baudelaire*. Translated by Martin Turnell. New York: New Directions, 1950.

Sieburth, Richard. "Poetry and Obscenity: Baudelaire and Swinburne." *Comparative Literature* 36 (Fall 1984): 343–53.

Spencer, Lloyd. "Allegory and the Commodity: The Importance of *Central Park*." *New German Critique* 34 (Winter 1985): 59–77.

Swain, Virginia E. "The Legitimation Crisis: Event and Meaning in Baudelaire's 'Le Vieux Saltimbanque' and 'Une Mort héroique.' " *Romanic Review* 73 (1982): 452–62.

Symposium 38, no, 3 (Fall 1984).

Vlasopalos, Anca. *The Symbolic Method of Coleridge, Baudelaire, and Yeats*. Detroit: Wayne State University Press, 1983.

Weinberg, Kerry. "The Women of Eliot and Baudelaire: The Boredom, the Horror and the Glory." *Modern Language Studies* 14, no. 3 (Summer 1984): 31–42.

Welch, Cyril, and Liliane Welch. *Emergence: Baudelaire, Mallarmé, and Rimbaud*. State College, Penn.: Bald Eagle Press, 1973.

Wing, Nathaniel. "The Danaides' Vessel: On Reading Baudelaire's Allegories." In *Pre-Text/Text/Context*. Edited by Robert J. Mitchell. Columbus: Ohio State University Press, 1980.

Wohlfarth, Irving. " 'Perte d'Auréole': The Emergence of the Dandy." *MLN* 85 (May 1970): 529–71.

Acknowledgments

"A Perfect Silence of the Will" (originally entitled "Baudelaire") by Georges Bataille from *Literature and Evil* by Georges Bataille, and translated by Alastair Hamilton, © 1973 by Calder and Boyars Ltd. Reprinted by permission. This essay originally appeared as *La littérature et le mal* in 1957 by Editions Gallimard, Paris.

"The Will to Ecstasy: The Example of Baudelaire's 'La Chevelure' " by Victor Brombert from *Yale French Studies* 50 (1974), © 1974 by *Yale French Studies*. Reprinted by permission.

"Poetry and Its Double: Two 'Invitations au voyage' " by Barbara Johnson from *The Critical Difference: Essays in the Contemporary Rhetoric of Reading* by Barbara Johnson, © 1980 by the Johns Hopkins University Press, Baltimore/London. Reprinted by permission.

"Exploding Poetry: Baudelaire" by Georges Poulet from *Exploding Poetry: Baudelaire/ Rimbaud* by Georges Poulet, translated and with an introduction by Françoise Meltzer, © 1984 by the University of Chicago. Reprinted by permission of the University of Chicago Press. This essay was originally published in Paris as *La Poésie éclatée: Baudelaire/Rimbaud* in 1980 by Presses Universitaires de France.

"Baudelaire's Creative Criticism" by Rosemary Lloyd from *French Studies: A Quarterly Review* 36, no. 1 (January 1982), © 1982 by the Society for French Studies. Reprinted by permission.

"Baudelaire: Portrait of the Artist in 1846" by Bernard Howells from *French Studies: A Quarterly Review* 37, no. 4 (October 1983), © 1983 by the Society for French Studies. Reprinted by permission.

"Insertion in an Oval Frame: Poe Circumscribed by Baudelaire" by Mary Ann Caws from *The French Review* 56, no. 5 (April 1983) and from *The French Review* 56, no. 6 (May 1983), © 1983 by the American Association of Teachers of French. Reprinted by permission.

"A Phantom" translated by Richard Howard from *The Flowers of Evil* by Charles Baudelaire, © 1982 by Richard Howard. Reprinted by permission of the author.

"Anthropomorphism and Trope in the Lyric" by Paul de Man from *The Rhetoric of Romanticism* by Paul de Man, © 1984 by Columbia University Press. Reprinted by permission.

"Temporality in Baudelaire" by Helen Regueiro Elam, © 1987 by Helen Regueiro Elam. Published for the first time in this volume. Printed by permission.

Index

Abraham, Karl, 10
Abyss, 151
Activity, 14–16, 21
Aesthetic dignity, 9
Allegory, 45
Also Sprach Zarathustra (Nietzsche), 15
"Âme du vin, L'," 88–89
"Amour et le crâne, L'," 82
Analogy, versus enumeration, 133
Anthropomorphism, 126–27, 132, 137, 142
Apostrophe, 30–31, 145, 147
Appalled/pall, as key terms, 107, 109, 110
Appearance, 121–22
Art: and economy of exchange, 48–51; for art's sake, 23, 96; as wagering, 88
Art de ne pas payer, L', (Balzac), 83–84
Art-ivresse. See Intoxication, aesthetics of
Atheism, 96
Au-delà (pure beyond), 72–73
Auerbach, Erich, 9
Augier, Emile, 47
Augustine, Saint, 64
"À une passante," 130, 131
Aurevilly, Barbey d', 85
Aurora borealis, 86
Avarice, language of, 47

"Balcon, Le," 76, 146–47, 148
Balzac, Honoré de, 84, 86
Baudelaire, Charles: on acting, 91–92; and articles for Crepêt's anthology, 85; on Banville, 36–37; on capital, 50–51; on correspondences, 44, 90; as critic, 81–90, 91–99; on doubt, 93–95; on the economy of the work of art, 49–51; and failure, 20, 24; on Fall from grace, 64; on the future, 72; on horror vs. ecstasy of life, 17; and Hugo, 1–2, 3–10; and letter to Ancelle (1866), 13; and letter to Hugo (1859), 5–6; on Le Vavasseur, 90; on lyricism, 37, 40; moral attitude of,

11–16; on nonconceptual arts, 98; and notice on Desbordes-Valmore, 89–90; on original sin, 64; as Poe critic, 73, 86, 87, 88, 90; as poet of irreparability, 67; and reframing of Poe's "The Oval Portrait," 101–23; and review of *Madame Bovary*, 84; and review of *Prométhée delivre*, 83; and "statue of the impossible," 20; on travel, 71, 152; on will, 20. *See also individual titles;* Death; Grammar; Lesbianism
Baudelaire's works: consciousness of self in, 63; "dream of stone" in, 17, 61, 62; intoxication in, 27, 28–30, 33; light in, 107–9, 110, 139; multiplication in, 29–30; narrative frame in, 101–5, 110–11, 116–19, 123; nature in, 130, 135; receding past in, 74–75; repetition in, 147; theme of the living dead in, 77–78; time in, 68–70, 118, 143–53
Beauty, 56; decayed, 67
Berenice (Poe, trans. Baudelaire), 120, 122
Bernard, Suzanne, 35–36, 37, 55
Black Tulip, The (Dumas), 52
Blin, Georges, 52, 60
"Blue Dahlia" (Dupont), 52
Bos, abbe du, 39
Byron, George Gordon, Lord, 3

"Cadre, Le," 114, 117
Champfleury, 85
"Chanson d'apres-midi," 86
"Chant d'automne," 84
Char, Réné, 14
Chateaubriand, 37
"Chevelure, La," 27–33, 145
Closure, 105–6, 108
Code, poetry as, 37, 61
Coleridge, Samuel Taylor, 3
Comme, 44, 45, 131–33, 137

RITTER LIBRARY
BALDWIN-WALLACE COLLEGE